A Corner in the N

Yesterday and To-day

with Border Folk.

A Corner in the North:

Yesterday and To-day

with Border Folk.

By

HASTINGS M. NEVILLE.

Rector of Ford, Northumberland

ILLUSTRATIONS BY HERBERT NEVILLE

FIRST PUBLISHED IN 1909.
Reprinted in reset type, 1998, by
LLANERCH PUBLISHERS.
FELINFACH

ISBN 1 86143 068 X

LIST OF ILLUSTRATIONS

PLATES (centre pages)

CONTENTS

PREFACE

In the following pages nothing more is attempted than a plain record of things heard and seen, by the writer, within a limited area on the English Border between the Tweed and the Cheviots.

What is said about the farming of former days, its economic conditions, and the contrast it presents to the farming of today, is entirely derived from statements carefully gathered from agricultural labourers themselves. The writer does not profess any special knowledge of farming matters, but has simply set down, as an onlooker, impressions derived from long residence in the district.

It has appeared to him no less than a duty for a clergyman living many years in so interesting a countryside, to record, as far as possible, the vanishing traditions of its people.

He desires to express his thanks to the many kind friends and neighbours who have assisted him with their reminiscences.

FORD RECTORY
January 4th, 1909.

A CORNER IN THE NORTH

Chapter I

Christmas and New Year

We have, sometimes in January, sometimes in March, what our weatherwise people of the countryside call a "feeding" storm. It begins with a hard frost, on which falls, some still night, five inches of fine snow. There is then a partial thaw, giving one the impression that we shall soon see hills and fields their own colour again, but to the observant eye the thaw is not complete. Lines of snow still lie under the weather side of the hedges and plantations; there will certainly be more snow, and plenty of it. There is the greatest difference in the world between a sudden and partial thaw, and a "right fresh", which comes to some purpose, when the snow has accumulated day after day until the storm has expended its force. Then there is a thaw indeed. It comes with a rushing steady blast of ice cold wind from the west. This wind, more by its force than by any warmth it conveys, perforates the snow drifts and wears them rapidly away, and then our roads are furrowed with rushing currents, our "burns" run full. Our river Till, usually so sluggish, is a mighty flood, and the valley, looked at from the neighbouring hills, seems to have returned to its primæval condition and become in great measure a glistening lake. The sun comes out, and we go down and stand on the ancient bridge to watch the swirling water as it comes thundering against the solid piers, and we smell the scent of the Cheviots brought down by the red water.

But this water flood, coming from the melting snow of the Cheviots and Glendale, although a striking evidence of the power of nature when she wills to have her way, is comparatively harmless.

It is the spring flood, caused by continuous rains, that is the dread of the farmer and the shepherd, especially in the low lying lands. When there are several days of heavy rain to make compensation for a dry winter, really dangerous floods occur. The Cheviot slopes first drink in enough to replenish the springs, and send the rest foaming down their glens and gullies to the tributaries of the Tweed. The floor of our valley, before of vivid green, dotted with sheep and lambs, and slowly moving herds of cattle, soon becomes as a sheet of burnished silver.

1

There has been some warning, because the burns always rise before the river is big, and the flocks are driven to safe pastures. But in some places dams are suddenly broken through, and flocks overwhelmed and washed away. Bridges are damaged and a wide resistless seething torrent as high as the tops of the hedges passes athwart the road that connects you with the outer world.

Some Old Customs

Until about five-and-twenty years ago the custom of Hogmanay existed in our village. This took the form of a round of visits made by the children on Old Year's Day. They would assemble at the front door, and, by way of greeting, sing with great gusto certain quaint catches, always including the following:-

Get up, guid wife and shake your feathers,
And dinna think that we are beggars;
We're little children come to play,
Please to give us our Hogmanay.
May God bless all friends and dear,
A Merry Christmas and Happy New Year.

The visit was paid first to the Castle, then to the rectory and the nearest farm houses, and then to the village. The children formed a lively group, the Red Riding Hood cloaks, which many of the girls wore, brightening the snowy landscape. Each child went away pleased with a coin, an orange, and a kind word. The term Hogmanay is not only applied to this custom, but to any gift received at the New Year or at Christmas, and is practically what is called in the South a Christmas Box.

The "first foot" in our village is generally Jack Frost, who comes with stealthy tread under bright starlight, and leaves the roads as hard as iron. The old custom of "first footing", which is a sort of house-to-house carnival in the early morning of New Year's Day, has almost entirely died out in our neighbourhood. This is chiefly owing to the decrease of the population. Village communities have become so much smaller that the people lose sight of their traditions, and have little left of that social feeling which is essential to the keeping up of old customs.

But while good fellowship may have lost something by the disappearance of first footing, sobriety must have made a considerable gain. Not many years ago every house in the village was open, in expectation of the first foot. The whisky bottle was much in evidence, each first footer carried one with

2

him, and another was ready on the table of the house visited, for an exchange of hospitalities between the host or hostess and the caller.

The first footer must, if possible, be one who was considered lucky, and it was sometimes arranged beforehand with the lucky one that he should be first to cross the threshold, and sometimes a small sum of money was paid to secure the visit. A woman, a fair man, and a flat-footed person were thought unlucky. It was considered a most ill-omened thing if the person first coming in should not bring in something and place it on the table, even if it were only a small piece of bread or a penny or even a piece of coal, and it was still more unlucky for anyone to carry anything whatever out of the house. Fire and water are not usually denied even to an enemy, but to give fire from the hearth on New Year's morning was a terrible thing, certain to bring disaster on the house. This, of course, dates from the days of the tinder box, before matches were invented, or "spunks" made by casual tramps in the village poor-house, for then it was the frequent custom of neighbours to borrow embers from one another to light their fires or candles.

Owing to the scarcity of young people in the village, there was no "guisering" at Christmas, 1903, although there were a few lads who intended to continue the custom, but whose courage failed them at the last moment. And so there passed away one of the most ancient of our customs, and undoubted relic of the old miracle plays. With careful handling one can imagine it might have been made the groundwork of simple dramatic representations in which the people might amuse themselves as of old, instead of depending for amusement on others.

Guisering began a few days before Christmas. The troupe consisted of about six or seven. They dressed themselves in the most outlandish fashion. Some wore over their other clothes a white shirt, with a leather belt around the waist. The headgear of the chief actor was a cocked hat, others wore tall hats shaped like an archbishop's mitre, the edges decked with ribbons, and the front decorated with small coloured pictures. They wore epaulettes of parti-coloured ribbons, or paper shreds. The leader carried a sword.

One heard uproarious laughter from the kitchen, and the sound of heavy boots on the cement floor. The lads one knew so well were so disguised that it was only their voices that revealed their identity. One dressed like a servant maid, and going by the name of Betty, begins the action of the play by sweeping the floor vigorously with a broom, and singing as a sort of prologue:-

> "Redd sticks, redd steels,
> Here comes in a pack of feels,
> A pack of feels behind the door,
> Step in, King George, and clear the way.

> "Make room for gallant sport,
> For in this house we must resort.
> Resort, sport, merry play,
> Step in, King George, and clear the way."

King George now comes forward and says:-

> "Here I come in myself, sir,
> That never came before;
> I'll do the best that I can do,
> What can the best do more.

> "The next that I call in,
> He is a farmer's son,
> He is like to lose his own true love,
> Because he is too young.

> "If I be too young,
> I've got money for to rove,
> And freely will I spend it all
> Before I lose my love.

> "The next that I call in,
> He is Goliath bold,
> He fought the battle of Quebec
> And won five tons of gold.

> "Here I come in Goliath,
> Goliath is my name,
> A sword and pistol by my side
> I hope to win the game.

> "Goliath, Goliath, it is not in your power,
> I plunge my dart into your heart
> And down your blood shall pour."

4

They begin to fight and one falls down dead.....

> "Now this young man is dead, sir,
> And on the ground is laid,
> And you shall suffer for it
> I am very sore afraid.
>
> "You being villains all,
> How can you set the blame on me,
> Surely my two eyes were shut
> When this young man did dee.
>
> "How could your two eyes be shut
> When I stood looking on,
> You drew your sword, gentle sir,
> And slain this young man.
>
> "If I have slain this young man,
> I will cure him in half an hour,
> Is there a doctor to be found here?"

One steps up, and says:-

> "I am a doctor-----"
> "What can you cure?"
> "I can cure the hitches, stiches, and billy-go-hitches-----"
> "What will you take to cure him?"
> "No, five pounds won't buy a pair of breeches for the devil
>   to fly up the lum with."
> "Will ten pounds do?
> "Yes, I've got a bottle here.
> I'll put a little in his nose and a little in his veins,
> Rise up, King George, and fight again."

King George then says:-

> "Once I was dead, sir,
> And now I am alive,
> Blessed be the happy man,
> That made me to revive.
> We will all shake hands,
> And we will fight no more;
> And we will agree like brothers,
> As we did once before."

5

Here they sing a few songs, and taking round a box to collect money, leave with good wishes to the host, saying:-

"Your bottles are full of whisky,
Your barrels are full of beer,
I wish you a Merry Christmas
And a Happy New Year."

The reference to the battle of Quebec is interesting, as there is a tradition that a Ford man, whose name I have not been able to find out, was with General Wolfe when he died.

Among the catches sung in the course of their performance was the following quaint ditty:-

How broad is your river, Mr. Carpenter?
The ducks and the geese they do swim over,
    Do swim over, do swim over,
The ducks and the geese they do swim over,
                Fal lal de dey.

How deep is your river, Mr. Carpenter?
Throw in a stone and it will soon find the bottom,
    Soon find the bottom,
Throw in a stone and it will soon find the bottom,
                Fal lal de dey.

Whose house is yon over yonder, Mr. Carpenter?
That house belongs unto the owner,
    Unto the owner, unto the owner,
That house belongs unto the owner,
                Fal lal de dey.

What clock is it, Mr. Carpenter?
Here's my watch and you may view her,
    You may view her, you may view her,
Here's my watch and you may view her,
                Fal lal de dey.

The memory of Hallowe'en (All Saints' Eve) celebrations only remains with our oldest people. They seem to have consisted of the amusing game of "snatch apple" - ducking for apples in a tub of water - and certain rather rough practical jokes. Boys would climb the thatched roofs of the cottages and throw turnips and cabbages down the chimney. Some of them

6

would fasten the door outside, blow smoke through the keyhole to give alarm of fire, and then decamp.

Another vanished custom still remembered was the "beating of the bounds." It applied to the estate, not the parish, and when dying out, it did not take place annually, but at longer intervals. It must have been a business-like thing, for it occupied two days. It was carried out by a few men and boys on foot. The boys were taken that they might learn what the exact boundaries were, and so remain witnesses of them to the end of their lives. One would have thought that the toil of walking so many miles would have been enough to produce a lasting impression on the poor lads, but it was the barbarous custom of those days to give the boys a beating at certain points in the perambulation, that they might have the geography of the estate more permanently impressed on their minds. Sometimes the punishment was still more cruel, the lads being deprived of food in the presence of a bountiful lunch supplied to the men.

The keeping of "Carling Sunday"(1) is remembered by some of our old folks. It was the fifth Sunday in Lent, called in the church "Passion Sunday." No doubt its observance as a social feast day had a religious origin, like the keeping of the fourth Sunday in Lent, called in the Church Mid-Lent and Refreshment Sunday, and celebrated in the Midlands by the eating of veal. It is by the social custom of feasting on fried peas that Carling Sunday was distinguished on the Borders fifty years ago. The custom still survives in Norham-on-Tweed.

It seems less strange that fried peas should have been considered quite a dainty dish, when one thinks that the usual food of the people at the time had but little variety. Possibly the dish, homely in its materials, may have been somewhat inviting. The carlings were field peas steeped in water until soft, and then fried in a "yetling" or pan with brown sugar, and rum or whisky, sometimes brandy. Large quantities of peas were steeped by the millers and given to their customers. The village inn was the scene of much feasting on the carlings, which were prepared and served gratuitously to all customers who came.

Easter is much observed with us as a Church festival. Whether from respect for the chief Sunday in the year, or simply from the following of old custom; every woman and child who comes to Church on Easter day wears some new article of clothing. But Easter Monday is a great day for the children of the village, for the rolling of Easter eggs goes on to-day as it has doubtless for many centuries. It is, of course, a custom common to European countries, but I would simply record the practice as it exists in this year 1908. Children are presented by their elders, friends, and the local tradesmen, with a great many coloured eggs. They are boiled quite hard and decorated with many devices and patterns. The children all assemble in a field having a steep slope and bowl the eggs uphill with as much force as they can. The object is to try whose egg will hold out longest without breaking; and sometimes, who can throw the egg furthest. In the old days broom and whin blooms were used to dye the eggs yellow. The patterns were traced on the egg with the pointed end of a rushlight. The grease preserved the pattern, while the egg was being dyed, and was afterwards rubbed off, leaving the decoration the natural colour of the shell. It is fitting that a custom connected with the great festival of the Resurrection should have survived when so many other customs have died out.

I find that the school children of Norham-on-Tweed play with a ball, striking it to the ground, and each time it rebounds saying a word of the following rhyme-

"Tid, Mid, Miseray,
Carlin', Palm, and Pace-egg Day"

by way of counting the Sundays in Lent as they look forward to the approach of Easter Monday with its holiday and rolling of Pace-eggs.

(1) Brockett says Carling Sunday was formerly denominated Care Sunday, which is Passion Sunday, as Care Friday and Care Week are Good Friday and Holy Week --- supposed to be so called from that being a season of great religious care and anxiety.

8

Chapter II

The Turn of the Year

The "turn of the year" is an expression often used in our border country, and it has a great deal of meaning with our people. For the turn of the year, from the old to the new, brings a change in the fortunes and prospects of a great many of our farm families.

It brings a change of masters, a change of home and scene, and often of occupation. The hirings for the year of service take place early in March, the actual removal in May, but the notice for ordinary hinds is given in February. This notice is termed "speaking." The farmer has, or has not "spoken." The stewards and shepherds, who have a higher office, and cannot so easily obtain new posts when there is to be a change, have a longer notice. The farmer "speaks" to them at the New Year, and they begin at once to look out for other situations, and generally obtain them, before the hirings come on. Those hands who receive no notice to leave are also spoken to, and make a fresh agreement to remain for another year. If the farmer does not speak they consider themselves discharged.

Stewards and shepherds are the most permanent hands on the farm. They are the most important to the farmer, and their position being more independent and responsible, they have not that inducement to change that affects the other hands. They often remain on one farm for ten years and more. When a shepherd leaves a master it is not seldom that he takes a small farm himself. He has not spent his money in many flittings, has accumulated a small capital, and his thorough knowledge of stock and grass is an asset of great value. The steward also manages sometimes to become his own master. It is a mistake to suppose that there is no prospect for a diligent and thrifty farm-worker. Undoubtedly, if there were more farms of a moderate size his prospect would be better; but our part of the country can show many an instance of farms successfully worked by the families of men who were once stewards, shepherds, or carters.

The system of hiring farm hands for the term of one year, with its consequent annual changes, is a very old and deeply rooted custom, and, although not unknown elsewhere, it prevails in its most

9

characteristic form in those counties adjoining the Border of Scotland on both sides.

It bears evident traces of an old nomadic trait in the character of the people. It would seem to be in the interest of the farmer that it ties down the worker for the whole course of the year's husbandry, but it releases him if desired at the end of the period, and although some hands remain, it begets a spirit of unsettledness in all. Many of our farmers, however, are tired of the yearly system, and would, if possible, adopt the monthly term of service, and a step towards this has been already taken in the payment of wages monthly instead of half-yearly as before. The people on the other hand, although beginning to dislike the annual changing, are on the whole inclined to adhere to the yearly engagement. They believe that the monthly system would cause more "shifting" than at present, and that, as the farm cottages are rent free, and so not free to be rented by disengaged hands, they might be at a disadvantage under it. They imagine, also, that the farmer might often be placed in a difficult position in case two or three families were to leave in turnip time or harvest.

Besides the free house, other parts of the wages in kind remain, such as the leading of the hind's coals, the use of his little garden plot, and its produce, and the usual 1,200 yards, or eighteen weighed bags, of potatoes. But all, or any of, these wages in kind could easily be commuted, and paid monthly in money.

It is quite possible that the monthly system might answer if it could be tried. Instead of making the hinds more restless, might not the very fact of the monthly notice on either side, and the greater difficulty of obtaining another place in a month, at an inconvenient time, perhaps, to the farmers of the district, be a check to rash action?

But it must be remembered that there is generally some radical reason for long standing industrial customs, either in the nature or circumstances of the people. With us it is not the single worker that we have to think of, as in a south country village which supplies men as the farmer needs them at a weekly wage, but we have to deal with families of workers, whose interests are bound up together, and who can obtain no home except at one of the limited number of cottages at a farm place.

So that the hind has to think not only of his own interests, but of the interests of each of his family, and especially of those of them who are hired to work. One working member of the family might differ with the master or steward, and that would "lift" them all and the people seem to think that once a year is enough to settle these little difficulties, which are not infrequent.

It should not be forgotten, in considering this question, that farming in the Border counties has been no haphazard thing, but, from what one knows of Northumberland and Berwickshire, it has been carried on, up to late years at least, with admirable energy, thoroughness and science. It would be impossible for our farmers to entrust their work to other than those experienced hands that have been trained to it in the family of the hind.

Curiously enough, the people themselves, who seem to think the monthly engagement would not suit them, strongly condemn the somewhat long delay between the time of notice and the actual flitting on the 12th of May of the hind who leaves. And they do so for this reason, which the writer has many a time heard them allege. The badly disposed hind, who has had some difference with the master or steward, will frequently take revenge by some act of mischief, which is difficult to bring home to him. It often, sad to say, takes the form of cruelty to the horses, and, it is to be suspected, the burning of corn stacks.

On the part of the workers there are many excellent reasons why they should sometimes migrate from farm to farm. Only a certain number of men and women are required by the farmer. He cannot engage all the members of the family, as they leave school, and are ready for work. If, therefore, a lad is ready for work, and is not required on the farm, the family must move to another place where he can be engaged. Sometimes the head of the family, who has worked for many years, is no longer equal to regular work. This makes one worker less in the family, and perhaps the farmer requires the full number. Another farm, therefore, must be sought where the father can remain free, and the rest of his family can supply the hands that are wanted.

But, of course, there are often very trivial and insufficient reasons for flitting. The hinds sometimes differ among themselves, although this does not often happen. There must also arise differences between master and servant, which makes it best that they should part. Cases occur in which a farm hand takes some

11

offence which is unsuspected by the farmer, and which he is never able to fathom. Where the demand for labour in the country is equal to, or greater than, the supply, which is not the case at present, men are often very reckless as to giving notice to leave. A farmer allowed one of his hinds to have the harness of his work-horses renewed because it was quite worn out. Another of his men having asked for new harness was refused, and at once gave notice to leave; although his harness was quite good.

Young men have often thrown up their situations because they have not had as many turns of station carting work as they liked.

It will generally be found, however, that the reasons for the migration of our farm people are good, and have to do with the advancement of the younger members of the family, as they become efficient workers. It is an error to call the present system of farm service in Northumberland the "bondage" system. The people themselves have put an end to what was called the "bond." This was an agreement made by the hind who was to inhabit one of the farm cottages, that in case he could not guarantee to the farmer as a worker another hand from his own family, he would provide one. This was generally a woman. She had board and lodging in the hind's house, and the hind paid her wages. This was the "bondager." Her lot was harder than that of the other women on the farm. She had to work for the hind in milking and house-work, and still do her full share of farm work. She was always more or less a stranger in the home, and nowhere is family life more exclusive than among our Border people. The sympathy of the people was always given to the hind in this case, because he had to pay a stated, or upstanding wage to the woman.

It was about sixty-four years ago that the dislike of the bondage system culminated in a determined attempt to put an end to it. The little market town of Wooler, situated at the foot of the Cheviots on the London Road, was the scene of one of the strongest protests of the hinds against the bond. It was on a hiring day in March. There was a large gathering of male and female workers from the whole of Glendale. The hinds wore a sprig of hawthorn in their hats, the carters a piece of whipcord, and the shepherds a tuft of wool, as emblems of their respective callings. Among the crowd mixed the farmers, who were looking around for likely hands to replace those who were leaving, and those hinds, who could not find a place without a bondager, were there to engage one.

An eye-witness of the scene says the people "were addressed from an upper window of an inn by a school-master who had espoused their cause, and of whom the prevailing cry was 'Another Moses come to lead the people.' Late in the day there was a great commotion in the Market Square; a farmer had engaged his hands leaving out the bondage condition. Others took the same course, and the bond was broken."

From that time the system gradually died out on the English border. Women workers remained, and to this day perform a great deal of the work of the farm, but they are engaged by the farmer, and work directly for him. It is a pity that the name bondager is still applied to them, for apart from the yearly engagement, which applies to all farm workers, they are not so much tied down as the men. The women have their wages only for the days they work, and not in sickness or bad weather when work cannot be done.

But although the women have not an upstanding wage, most of our farmers are very considerate in finding suitable work for them, even when bad weather interferes with their regular work.

There are women engaged on some farms who receive a house as part of their wages; their coals are carted, and they are allowed potatoes enough for the year. These women are termed "cottars." Within the memory of many living in our district two most important economic changes have taken place: one, remembered by our aged people, the commutation of the parson's tithe, the other, the payment of the bulk of the farm wages in money instead of corn. The payment of tithes in kind was no doubt a cumbersome method of rendering the Church her dues and the method of its collection often caused much friction between the clergy and their parishioners; but as long as it lasted, and that was for many centuries, it was a plan not unsuited to the condition of the country. For the country supplied its own wants, ground its own corn, exchanged one commodity for another, and was to the fullest extent self dependent.

And so also with the hind's wages. He received an actual share of the fruits of the farm, in the shape most suited to his surroundings. Seventy years ago men's wages were during the year £4 in money, and twelve and a half bolls of corn of different kinds, namely, six of oats, four of barley, two of beans, and half a boll of wheat: also half a stone of wool, and the keep of a cow, in grass in summer, and one ton of hay in winter. When the hind was not able to buy a cow, the farmer provided one during the man's term of service. It was called a "put on" cow. The wages included 1,000 yards of potatoes, the farmer planting and carting them home, the hind supplying the seed, and taking them up in his own time. Each hind had to rear some chickens for the farmer at his cottage. His wife had to shear corn in harvest in lieu of house rent, and in addition to this she was required to spin so many hanks of lint for the farmer's wife. One woman worker was always supplied by the "full hind." She was paid only in money at the rate of eightpence a day in winter, tenpence in summer, and a shilling a day for twenty days in harvest.

Loose or "daytilman" men received nine shillings a week, and a gift of £1 in harvest. Young men driving a pair or horses got one shilling a day. Learners, boys and girls, went to work at ten years of age, and received fourpence a day. The amount of corn paid as wages varied with its price. At this time the price of a boll, or six bushels of wheat, was thirty shillings, of barley fifteen shillings, and of oats twelve shillings. Beef and mutton were from fourpence to fivepence per pound.

There has been but little change in the hours of labour. The people on the land have the longest work hours of any class of workers. Their work begins in winter with the dawn and ends at dusk. In spring and summer they begin at six, and end at six, with two hours and a half for their meals, this interval including time for breakfast and dinner. No time is now allowed for tea, except in harvest and hay time. There used to be a meal that went by the name of "dounder time," between dinner and supper, called in Scotland "four hours." The time occupied by the men in feeding and yoking the horses in the morning, and the taking them to the farm stable after work and feeding and "fettling" them in the evening, is additional work, which in the morning makes it necessary for the men to rise at half-past four in summer and an hour before daybreak in winter.

There is no Saturday half-holiday for the field worker. The young man driving a team of cart horses cannot forbear halting by the hedge side and watching wistfully the football team from the neighbouring town of Wooler, playing a match with the lads of Crookham. He has the sad thought that games are not for him, while he is hired on the land. Can he be blamed for sometimes resolving to change his trade at the end of his year of service, and obtain greater freedom?

Making every allowance for the exigencies of agricultural work, which includes the care and feeding of animals, would it be too much to ask that one afternoon in the week should be given to those whose working hours are so long and laborious? This would be a great boon, especially to those who engage themselves to feed the cattle during a great part of Sunday. The half-holiday need not be on Saturday, indeed a Saturday holiday would be impossible on our farms, as on that afternoon all the food must be prepared and placed ready in the byres for the cattle, and in the fields for sheep, for use on Sunday. There is no doubt that a weekly half-holiday for the farm worker is a difficult problem, but some solution of it will soon be found. ·

Although the system of the yearly engagement of farm families will probably continue for some time longer, the old custom of public hirings is dying out. Men and women no longer feel inclined to stand in the market place or street of the country town, and wait until the farmer may chance to engage them.

It is quite unnecessary that they should do so, for the plan of advertising is much better, and now very often adopted. It gives both master and hind time to make enquiry about one another, while to engage a stranger in the hirings is often disastrous. No doubt the holidays which the March hirings involve are enjoyed by the young people, for they have many of the accompaniments of a fair, but, although the farmer does not seem to grudge the time, the plough is often left idle in the field for more than one day while the ploughman goes from hiring to hiring seeking a place.

It must here be said that there are some parts of the women's work which are, to say the least, quite unsuited for them, and which as yet machinery has done nothing to alleviate. It is considered specially the work of women to clean out the cattle byres, which no doubt they do keep in splendid order. It is their part also to turn over the vast heaps of manure that are stacked in the field in the winter.

Very painful it is to see them at work in the moist alley formed by the streaming walls of stuff which they fork from side to side. The state of their clothes when they return home may be imagined.

15

The same remarks will apply to their employment in sowing guano in the turnip furrow, and to the heavy, continuous, and suffocating work of feeding the thrashing machine with sheaves.

It is difficult to see why these unpleasant and less healthy employments should he thought more suited for women than for men. They are no easier than ploughing, sowing corn, harrowing the land or driving horses.

It would be unfair to begin all at once to condemn employers for the existence of this order of things. Both employers and employed have become so accustomed to the system that they do not realize how objectionable it seems to an outsider; indeed, the men on a farm would probably refuse to do the work that it has so long been customary for women to do One cannot but believe however, that it will very soon be seen that in farm labour, as in factories and mines, the work must be suited to the worker.

There should be a readjustment of women's work on farms, not by legislation, but preferably by mutual agreement, and, while their wages can never be expected to equal the wages of men, as their labour in its nature and amount must always be different from that of men to the world's end; yet, while paid less, their wages as yearly servants should be "upstanding," that is, regular and irrespective of weather conditions, and they should have the same advantage as men in time of sickness.

Of course such changes must to some extent arise from the demand of the workers themselves, but they will be slow in coming unless the process is assisted by public opinion and a growing sense of the fitness of things.

16

CHAPTER III

Porridge and Milk

The commutation of "the boll," that is to say, of corn wages into money, arose from the changing condition of the times. It was adopted gradually, but soon became general. The possession of money wages gave greater freedom. It was far more convenient, and although at first it may have led to extravagance in those not accustomed to dealing with money, it enabled the thrifty to manage their earnings to much greater advantage than when the meal chest served as the family purse. The people certainly consider themselves immeasurably better off now than they were in the days when their corn was the medium of exchange, and they were greatly in the hands of the miller and the travelling provision merchant.

But from this, as in all general improvements, there followed some unfortunate results, as many of the older people regretfully admit. The improvement of the cottages which has taken place at all our farms, and which was so much needed, has, of course, tended to oust the cow. The entry of the cottage often had a cow byre below and a bed above. The cow was an inmate close at hand. A man of eighty four told me that when young, he could touch the cow's back as he lay in bed. It was a different thing when the cow had to be kept in the farmer's byre. The cow, which was an institution with every cottager, has almost disappeared from our farms and villages. When it was "put on," as part of a man's wages, even those who could not afford to buy a cow were able to keep one. A slight deduction was made from the man's wages, the farmer supplied grazing and hay, and had the calves. In the case of the man who owned his cow, the cow's feed was included in the wages, and the calf of course belonged to the man.

There are still some persons in our village who remember that almost every one of the cottagers owned a cow, and reared one or more calves to sell at a good price when two years old. As many as seventy cows and heifers were driven out to the Common each morning, and home again each evening, by the village cowherd.

The proprietor of the estate supplied the people with cow byres at a nominal rent; and also with a field in the village, for temporary use, at ten shillings a year for each beast.

17

Why, then, is it that only one family in the village keep cows now, and that milk is often not to be obtained? There is only one answer to this question. The great blow to cow keeping was the enclosure of the parish Common. By this act all rights of grazing were taken away from our villagers, and a mere remnant of the Common, amounting to five acres, was generously conferred upon the parish for a recreation ground, and all the rest annexed to the adjoining estates. It is quite true that the Common land had been made a camping ground for muggers and gipsies, who used to graze their horses upon it and who sometimes tried to claim it as a permanent home; but surely this abuse might have been remedied without depriving our people of their ancient rights. There were other changes in operation which made it difficult for the villagers to continue the practice of keeping cows. Corn became cheap and the farmer began to grow less of it. They were therefore unable to give straw, as they always used to do with great liberality, to the people in exchange for manure, and they became less and less willing gratuitously to assist the villagers with their horses and ploughs to cultivate their allotment strips, that they might grow straw and hay for themselves.

But the disappearance of the cow at the farm places had quite another cause. This was due to the commutation of corn wages into money. Before this great change the farmer and the hind worked together in this matter, and in others, more than they do at present, for their mutual advantage. With money wages in hand, the hind grew more and more inclined to be free from any joint arrangement as to the cow, which belonged to the old system of payment in kind. The arrangement as to the cow, whether "put on," or fed as part of the wages, tied him down for the year. And there were often difficulties; cows do not give milk all the year round, and some cows are better than others. These details were not always considered when the hiring took place, but were apt to cause trouble afterwards.

When once the hind had sold his cow, he did not often feel inclined to buy another. There were so many things that money would buy; tea was becoming cheaper, and cheese, which had been troublesome to make, could be got at the shop. The hind's wife, too, who had in the past laboured so hard at dairy work, sharing in the feeling of independence that money wages gave, professed to be

18

tired of the cow, would not be at the pains to milk it, and was not sorry to give it up; and there was money to buy butter. Our people when referring to those times often quote an old homely proverb which says "a cow and a clout is soon run out," by which they imply that when once you have sold your cow, the money you receive for it will soon dwindle, and you are not likely to buy another. Old farm friends who had for some time been separated by "flittings" would on meeting again, accompany the hearty handshake with the inquiry, "How's your mother and the cow?"

It is not the fault of the farmer that his hinds have as a rule given up cows. He is generally most willing to meet his men liberally in this matter, and in our larger farms we still find perhaps one of the cottagers who has a cow, on the old system, either as a possession, or a loan with a corresponding reduction of money wages. It is the opinion of our people that the farmers were very hard hit when payment in money took the place of payment in kind, and certainly, as to cow keeping, the farmer would not feel the cost of grazing and feeding his servants' cows as much as he would the paying out of the equivalent of this in money, which on an average was three shillings a week.

But it is the bearing of this matter on the question of the food of the people which is so important. It is acknowledged on all sides that they have more freedom of action, and are better housed and better clothed, than in the old days; but if we ask, "Are they better fed?" the answer must be decidedly in the negative. The possession of money has blinded them to the importance of the food question. They have got away from meal, milk, and cheese, and in great measure from the good home fed bacon which used to be their pride as it hung from the rafters of their houses. These things formed wholesome and strength-giving food, which they knew very well how to prepare: and now they are launched upon an expensive and insufficient diet, which very few of them are able to cook. It consists of an intermittent supply of butcher's meat, potatoes which fortunately still exist, tea, always taken without milk, and well steeped, and the ever present tin of Swiss milk for the baby. Thank God the people still bake their own bread in Glendale, and the aroma of it as they shift their sweet smelling loaves in the oven, or lay them in a goodly row, sloped against the edge of the bread board, is quite delightful.

But the disuse of porridge and milk is a lamentable and irreparable loss, as the older people freely admit; and the pale faces of the children and of the women workers in the fields plainly testify. Porridge was the staple food, and was taken for breakfast and supper, and being easily portable, was taken out into the field in harvest time. It is well known that porridge is much nicer when made in large quantities, as it was in harvest time; for then it was prepared in a shed, in a large cauldron, with a fire under it. The stick with which it was well stirred was hung from the roof, and descended into it, and thus the labour was lightened for the hand that merely had to move it round and round.

A parishioner tells me that she used to send out the porridge to the reapers, and she still has the round open wooden tub called the "fivesome boy," which contained enough for the four shearers and the bindster on the "foursome rig." She remembers sending out eighteen "fivesome boys" full of porridge at a time, with five tins of milk, and five wooden spoons. Each set of shearers lay around their "fivesome boy," in the most orderly way, in the oriental manner. All ate out of the same tub, each one selecting her own spot in the tub, without encroaching on her neighbour's portion. On the last day of harvest apples were concealed in the porridge, and each person would try to help herself where she thought an apple would be likely to be found, on the principle of the coins concealed in a Christmas pudding.

But this reminiscence shows how well the porridge must have been cooked. It was evidently firm and good, so that each person could cut it with a spoon. This was the only kind of porridge that would content the Irish harvesters, who were largely employed at that time. They were most difficult to please in the matter of cooking. Their idea of porridge was that it should he hard enough "for a cart wheel to go over it" or "to drive a little pony over it dry shod." There was a trick which the farmer's cook often played them; in order to stiffen the porridge she would stir some fresh meal into it after it was cooked and before serving it up

Even thirty years ago you could hardly go into any farm cottage without seeing the porridge in the pot on the fire, or on the table ready for the meal. To-day you never see it in the cottage being cooked or eaten, indeed it is rarely mentioned unless you yourself as a visitor speak about it. And no doubt one reason for its disuse was the giving up of cows. Porridge without milk is insipid, but with good new milk is delicious and nourishing.

But, curiously enough, this is not the reason the people now give you for its disappearance. It is strange, but true, that although they quite well know its value as a food, it is under a bann, they despise it. So long was it their food in the days of the meal chest and "small money," that now they foolishly discard it, even where milk is to he had, in testimony of their idea of freedom; their view being that the money payment of their wages has delivered them from serfdom. They neither know, nor would care to know, that my lord and his lady have it daily for breakfast, and that it appears on the tables of the best hotels in every part of the world. A little dialogue in which one of the speakers was a countryman of our district will show the feeling of the people on this subject.

"Now porridge is a good, cheap, wholesome food."

"But naebody eats them now."

"Why not? The people are not the men they were because they have given up porridge and milk."

"Oh, but they wadna' eat them now."

"Why not?"

"They 'wadna' be seen eating them now."

"Why ever not? We have it every morning."

"Aye, but ye're off the road."

"Off the road, what do you mean? What difference can that make?"

"Oh, well, it's a'right' for 'ee for naebody can see ye!"

"Well, but, good gracious! why shouldn't you be seen?"

"Oh, well, a' I ken is, there's naebody about here wad eat parritche except a'hint drawn blinds."

No one who understands the way our people lived sixty years ago, and how they live now, can doubt that their present food is much less abundant and less nourishing than it was. In the days of cow keeping, cheese was made in every house, and laid up in store. Families used to act on the co-operative principle. In order to make the cheese of perfectly fresh milk they clubbed their milk together. Each family had its cheesemaking day, and four or five cottagers would contribute their milk to the cheese that was being made on

21

that day, and so the turn of each household would come round, and in time several good cheeses, made from perfectly sweet milk, were stored up, as a substantial and wholesome addition to the food supply of each family. Fourteen or fifteen good sized cheeses were sometimes stored by one cottager for winter use. Both ewe's and cow's milk were used, and were often mixed together.

When we think of the great value of cheese as a food, it is sad that it has almost entirely disappeared from the cottager's table. To buy it at the shop is so very different a process from cutting it from your own ample store, knowing that it is made in the best way, and is of the best quality. But the days of cottage cheese-making are gone. All that remains to call to mind the custom is the solid block of stone you sometimes see outside the cottage and near the door. This was the primitive cheese press.

The giving up of his cow by the cottager not only tended to discourage the use of porridge and to make an end of cheese-making, but also to deprive the people of what they always considered their greatest dainty, the "girdle cake," popularly called "Neddy." It was made of flour, cream and fresh butter kneaded, without yeast, then rolled out to the size of the "girdle" or round iron plate hung over the fire. It was about half an inch thick, and when ready for use it was cut up into squares and piled on plates. The turning of this large round cake that both sides might he equally baked, required much dexterity and quickness. When a friend came unexpectedly from a distance, to put on a girdle cake was the only resource of hospitality, and when the housewife wished to give a treat to the youngsters she would accede to their frequent request to bake a "Neddy."

Girdle cakes are still made, with lard instead of cream but not often; indeed with the narrow ranges now put into cottages there is not room for the old girdle to hang, the little ovens on one side of the fire and the round pot on the other, shoulder it out.

In very few cottages do you now see the ancient "crook." It was perforated with a number or holes, one above another, for the regulation of the height of the pot, kettle, or girdle as they hung above the fire. Indeed the less ancient "swey," an improved kind of crook which moves on a pivot, although still used in many cottages, is passing away. These old fashioned arrangements which date from the time before ovens round or square were in use in the cottages, had advantages which nothing has replaced. With the "swey" meat could be roasted before the fire bars, as it always should be, and the old crook helped to bake all the bread. Then it was good English barley meal and pease that made the people's bread, and it was all baked on the girdle. It was made either in small round "bannocks," or in large thick loaves the size of the girdle. The bread, when cooked on both sides, was removed from the girdle and placed on an iron bracket and gradually turned, so that the edges might be cooked before the fire. When quite done the loaves were all placed in a wooden rack made with open bars hanging from the ceiling and called a "flake." There is perhaps nothing that makes one better realize the actual feeling of the people seventy years ago about their food than the gusto with which the aged ones speak of the days when white wheaten bread was their greatest treat and luxury, eaten when they went out to tea and at Christmas time. But the white bread of those days was made from good English wheat, grown and ground in the parish, and taken from the cottager's own store. It was indeed "the bread of carefulness," but it was all the sweeter for that. The bakers tell us now that you cannot make bread of English wheat. Certainly not the bread they make, but bread far more nourishing and palatable. The worst madness of the present day is to study appearances and fashion in food, rather than its nourishing qualities. Our arable land is now fast going back to pasture; this is no greater change than that which will probably succeed it, when England may be only too glad to eat its own good wheaten bread once more.

CHAPTER IV

"The May"

"Thou tellest my flittings; put my tears into thy bottle: are not these things noted in thy book."---Ps. lvi. 8.

These words from the Prayer Book version of the Psalms came suddenly into my mind today as I was cycling along the road to Wooler. Flock after flock of ewes and lambs were making their way at intervals along the road with a great deal of bleating, but not such a painful bleating as on the sad day when the lambs arc first weaned from their mothers and sent to other pastures. Some of these flocks were moving very slowly forwards, others were at rest, feeding on the fresh spring grass by the roadside, some of the lambs lying in the very middle of the road. The shepherd of each resting flock with his plaid over his shoulder also rests on the sunny side of the road, sheltered from the north-west wind blowing keenly, by the green thorn hedge as yet unsullied by dust. He smokes his pipe, and sits a good while in the same place, but he is not tired, he is too wiry for that. He rests with a purpose - the flock has ten miles before it, and he knows that means ten hours of lingering travel, for the proverb, "the more haste the worse speed," specially applies in the work he is doing.

They are not hill sheep he is driving, they are far too quiet for that; indeed hill sheep belong to the hills, and stay there, even when there comes a change of owners, for it is doubtful if they would take to other land. Just as on the larger farms in Scotland, being taken over with the farm at a valuation, so hill sheep have not the trouble of flitting, nor the weariness of long travel over dusty roads, nor the sorrow of leaving their old haunts and settling down in strange pastures among unknown dangers. How little we know and think of the anxieties and responsibilities of other peoples' trades and callings. Talk an hour with a shepherd of our valley about his work, and you will perceive more than you have dreamt before of the scope and also the nobility of his occupation, you will see why his employment has from the remotest ages so fully typified the office of the King, the Teacher, the Saviour of men.

It is a good feeding ground this wayside pasture. The collies keep a good look out on the outskirts of the flock, and the shepherd's ear is alive to the hoot of the motor car. He has time, however, for a leisurely smoke and a good crack with a passing friend on the subject of the May farm sales, for, be it known, it is our May Day.

Our May Day is not the first of the month with its romance of maidens going forth to bathe their faces in the early dew, nor is it the 29th, the oak apple day of the South, of which one has dim memories of village processions, men in white ducks carrying gorgeous may-poles, and the May Queen in a flowery sedan chair with gilded oak apples and a band of music. We have no May Day of this sort. Our May Day is not quite a day of joy, and although fraught with many important consequencies to our people, and full of interest to the families of our country side, it cannot be said to savour of romance. Still it brings about many a pathetic scene, many a sad farewell is spoken. With us the 12th of the month is so important a crisis in the life of our agricultural families that it is always called by them "The May". It is well if that day dawns brightly and with good omens, for it is the great day which terminates and begins the annual term for which our farm workers are hired, the date from which, and to which, all their calculations are made; above all, it is the day of "flitting" from farm to farm of those who for various reasons find it desirable to make a change of place and master.

The flocks we saw by the wayside are only changing their pasture because their owners have taken other farms. We feel for the tired lambs when we think of the long road they have to go. There is indeed something pathetic in the flitting of the flocks to new pastures, but this feeling is dismissed when we observe the care of the shepherd, bringing his flock on to the new farm by easy stages, and long rests, and food by the way, and suiting his leisurely gait to theirs.

But there is real sadness in the sight of the annual migration of so large a proportion of our farm families. Perhaps the people themselves do not, at the time, feel the sadness of it, they are too busy, and there is the excitement of going to a new home, where prospects may be better for their young people; but to see our roads from morning to evening thronged with carts piled with the furniture and bedding of a large portion of our population, is a strange sight even

25

if you have seen it year after, year for a long time. It is one of the things which has not changed with other changes, a long-established custom, and it is hard to say how it can be altered. It is a rough but practical way of adapting the amount of labour to the demand for it, and of meeting the want of work for young lads and girls coming to a working age.

READY FOR FLITTING.

The farmer, as a rule, calculates the amount of labour he requires to the last ounce and hires his people accordingly, keeping some families, and parting with others. There is little of sentiment about the matter on either side. To the head of a family, his growing up sons and daughters represent a considerable income in the future, and no chance is lost of adding a few shillings a week to it by shifting to a new farm, where another of the girls who has left school can enter upon field work, or a lad is ready to take charge of a pair of horses; so that it is difficult to see how this system of yearly hiring and flitting can be changed for the better.

The annual exodus is a sad thing in many ways. It is sad because it means the negation of the idea of home. It keeps the people in a restless unsettled state of mind. The clergy find it a great obstacle

26

to their work, for no sooner do they become acquainted with the people, and the people settle down as churchgoers, than they have to say good-bye to them, and welcome and visit those who take their place. Congregations are unsettled long before the fatal day, and for some time after you do not get regular attendance from the farms. It is needless to say that the same effect is seen in our schools.

Our teachers lose many of their best pupils, and have to begin after a week's holiday, which is required for the people to get settled in their new homes, with many new scholars. Thus our farm children lose the benefit of continuity of teaching and influence both in church and at school.

Photo by]   [*J. Rule, Ford.*

THE FLITTING.

Of course there may be advantages on the other side in this system of annual hiring. It is often for their worldly benefit. It is a change of scene and society, making their lives a little less narrow and monotonous; indeed it is the only change they get. The flitting itself, too, laborious as it seems, and uncomfortable, unless it is exceptional May weather, is of great sanitary value, giving the opportunity for a thorough house cleaning and airing of the household goods. But it is sad nevertheless. There they go, cart

27

after cart, passing up the bank as we call our hill, the furniture in one cart, piled to a dangerous height, with the grandfather clock lying length wise and risking its life on the top. The people themselves consider the flitting a sorrowful time. They lose the companionship of those with whom they have worked for many years and with whom often a close friendship has arisen. Strangers take the place of those who have gone, and our Border folk are not good at making friends with new comers. With the shifting of, say, four out of its ten families, the whole farm hamlet is upset and torn asunder; and not only is its social life shaken, but the farm work is for a time a good deal disorganized, until the new hands fall into their places, and settle down, each to his own special work.

Many are the questions asked among the old hands about the new. Concerning one family it will be "How are they at the sowing?" and with regard to another, "How are they it the spreading of the muck?. It is always known among them when a thoroughly good hind is coming to a farm; quite as high a reputation can be gained for good hinding as for any other calling in any station of life.

In the second cart are the women and children seated on the bedding, caring for the caged canary, and the cherished pelargonium which had grown in the cottage window, and the arum lily now disconsolate with its glossy leaves drooping, and waving sad farewell. Poor little Sunday scholars. I wonder if you will come in for the school treat in the parish for which you are bound. Let us be thankful for the parochial territorial system of the Church of England, the only system by which the wandering scattered sheep and lambs of God's flock can be sought and gathered in and tended. One flitting on the road today afforded a remarkable instance of the meeting of past and present. There were two trucks, one piled with furniture, the other carrying the family and small belongings drawn by a traction engine. It was certainly a novelty, and the children seemed to be mightily enjoying the experience.

Our farms are very large and isolated, each one forming a small hamlet of itself. The hands who work them are not drawn from the villages. This self-contained system must needs have a narrowing effect upon the minds of the workers; but the bicycle, which almost every farm lad possesses, has of late years done much to counteract the depressing effect on the workers of spending their little leisure

28

on the scene of their day's labour, and only among their fellow workers. The worst is that Sunday is naturally the only day available for cycling to see distant friends, and many of our young people have yet to learn that a good cycle ride on Sunday need not prevent their going to church once in the day at least.

It is a lovely day for the flitting, a very fortunate circumstance, for our May Day is often cold and showery, and the people's bedding gets wet, and rheumatism makes a bad beginning in the new farm. All the fields are deserted, as horses and men are all busy with the flittings, but they look neat and trim with the young corn just giving the ruddy earth a soft tinge of green, except the fields left for turnips and potatoes, the work which is begun in earnest after the May. The idea one gets is that the spring labour has been finished in preparation for this day of change and pilgrimage.

In the time when cows were generally kept, last but not least in importance was the flitting of that good friend of the family, the cow. The good housewife was very careful over her cow, and, unless the journey was too long, she led her every step of the way to the new home; indeed the leading home of the cow was quite a ceremony; the woman, knowing that she would meet many acquaintances on the road, rigged herself out in her best clothes, and proud of her charge, if the cow was a good one, she was determined to present as respectable an appearance as possible on arriving at the new farm.

Holiday attire was and is now generally worn by the women and children as they sit among the straw and "plenishings" in the short cart which brings up the rear of each little procession. In our countryside carts are of two kinds only; the short cart which carries about 15 cwt., and has closed sides and a back for carrying coal, etc., and the long raft with rails at the sides and front for carrying sacks of corn, hay, timber and other bulky materials. These carts are admirably adapted to our hilly country. They rest on two wheels so that the goods they carry can be well balanced to the relief of the horse, and the same pair of wheels serves for both kinds of cart.

We never see such a thing as the heavy four-wheeled waggon of the South, the only approach to this being the flat railway and brewers' drays or "lorrys" that come out from the towns. Nor do we now see such a thing as a covered cart, but the old carriers, who have become extinct since the advent of railway trains, used them here. The last carrier on our main road was very deaf, and sitting inside his tunnel of canvas it was almost impossible to get him to make way for a carriage coming behind him.

Not so many years ago we used to be content to take our people to picnics, and even confirmations, in our carts kindly lent by the farmers for the purpose, and nicely furnished with straw seats. It was a slow process, but in summer time very enjoyable, and rendered possible many a holiday excursion which the expense of hiring carriages now forbids to those far from a railway station.

I was told that one woman was known to wear the same hat with a conspicuous white feather at every flitting of her family. She seemed to keep it specially for this purpose, as she never wore it at other times. Over the period of twenty years, in which the family made several removals, the hat and feather were in evidence on each occasion.

As may be supposed, the leading of the cow to her new home was sometimes a long weary journey, but when the distance was too great for one day the woman would arrange beforehand to spend the night at the house of some friend or acquaintance on the road.

On reaching the new home and before the family settle down, the first thought of the women is to paper the walls, and whitewash the ceilings. This they consider their own peculiar work with which indeed the men wisely do not interfere. It is pleasant to see the pride they take in this work, and how they appreciate any admiration by a visitor of the pattern of the paper and the arrangement of the pictures. And those pictures how interesting to see Robert Burns in close proximity to the benign countenance of Pius X. in full pontificals, and to know that whatever our Presbyterian population may still retain of their old Calvinistic principles, they have as little prejudice against religious pictures of a Roman type on their walls, as against the Jew pedlar, who comes around year by year to the newly-arrived cottagers, and drives a thriving trade with tinselled Madonnas, lovely landscapes, and portraits of the King and Queen.

Chapter V.

Sowing and Stacking.

At the annual hirings, among other questions the farmer asked before engaging a hind was, "Can you stack and sow?" These two operations of agricultural work are naturally of the utmost importance, for bad sowing frustrates all the previous labour on the land, and bad stacking may greatly mar the quality of the harvested crop. If the hind can sow and stack he is able to obtain a shilling or two a week more than one who cannot. In the old days the extra reward was half a boll of wheat. Even with the various machines with which sowing is very generally done at present, we are able to speak of hand sowing as still existing in some farms on both sides of the Tweed; indeed in Scotland it still prevails to a very large extent. Hand sowing will no doubt soon become one of the lost arts. Old as the human race itself, bringing down with it through the ages a thousand associations of human interest and divine teaching, the passing away of hand sowing cannot but be a matter of regret to every thoughtful mind. The machine may in time be made to do as well, but there is something noble, and which cannot be replaced, in the figure and action of the sower, striding with measured step along the furrows, and with a regular sweep of his outstretched arm, casting an even rain of seed upon the soil.

As ploughing is considered the lightest labour of the field, so sowing, contrary to what the mere onlooker would suppose, is the hardest. It is heavy' work for two reasons; first because of the roughness of the ground to be traversed, and then because of the weight of seed corn the sower has to carry in the sheet or apron gathered up and supported by his left arm. And the labour is continuous, several harrows with powerful horses following the sower pretty closely. It is the boast of experienced sowers how they could keep ahead of many harrows.

Sowing with both hands, which is still practised on both sides of the Tweed to some extent, is, of course, much more difficult and laborious, and few men have ever been able to do it well Both hands must in this case be free. It is therefore necessary to have a basket or "skep" fitted around the front of the body, and in this a double weight of seed is carried. The sower, thus heavily laden, moves forward deliberately, casting the seed aside each way, with right and left hand alternately, thus doing the work of two men, and sowing a double breadth of land across the field. In the case of the single-handed sower, a cast is made with every other step, but in that of the two handed sower, a cast is made with every step, the steps being more deliberate in the latter case, to allow time for both hands to perform the two movements of taking the grain from the skep and casting it. An inhabitant of one of our villages tells me that his brother, once a very strong man, quite broke down his health with double-handed sowing, when he was steward of Humbledon Buildings, a farm on the side of Humbledon Hill, a spur of the Cheviots with very steep fields.

One great advantage of hand sowing is that the quantity of seed can be regulated by the experienced sower to suit the quality of the land, which often differs in different parts of the same field. It is claimed, however, that the implement called the "fiddle," now most generally used for holding and casting the seed, has the same advantage, and that it can be adjusted to suit the quality of the land, It also imitates the two-handed sower by casting the seed on both sides at once. It certainly reduces the labour of the hands, but not the strain of carrying the weight of seed, or of walking over the ground.

The "fiddle" also has a disadvantage on a hill-side field, which no alteration in its construction or the method of using it can overcome. It is worked by the hand in exact time with the advancing foot. In going up against a hill the sower walks with a shorter step, and in slower time, than on level ground, or in descending a hill. At each step the same quantity of seed is released, but it falls on a smaller extent of the strip that is being sown, and therefore is too thick on the land when, on the other hand, the sower is going down the hill, his step is longer and quicker, and the space sown with each pull of the "fiddle" bow is much greater, and therefore the land is too thinly sown. It is impossible to rectify this by any further act on the part of the sower In using the "fiddle" the sower walks once along the middle of the five yard strip, and the seed flowing out on both sides, sows the whole breadth at once. In single-hand sowing, the sower casts the seed over the same breadth twice; once as he walks along one side, and again as he returns along the other side. In this way the work is very thoroughly done, and in a hilly field he is able to regulate the amount of seed he takes up and casts, to suit his uphill or downhill walk, and the length and time of his steps.

Machinery will, of course, be more and more applied to agriculture, and the hand of man will be less and less used. But while the advantage of this change may seem considerable, the loss on the other side should not be forgotten. An ancient handicraft like sowing, for instance, had reached perfection in the experienced sower. There was intelligence and conscious skill in every casting of the seed. The machine kills this handicraft, and puts in its place a number of mechanical experiments, which may succeed in the end, but in the meantime are often productive of much waste and disappointment. And although it is true that most of the hinds on our farms, instead of objecting to machinery, as they did at first, now welcome it as making their labour lighter, still it is really the case that the rapid lessening of hand work is the chief cause of the depopulation of our rural districts. The labour on all our farms is already reduced far below what is good for the land, but if, for example, a machine were introduced that would single turnips satisfactorily, another large reduction of farm hands would at once take place.

The hind who had any ambition to get on in his calling would not long rest content until he could stack as well as sow. I speak of the craft of stacking almost as a thing the past. There are, of course, still stacks of corn at every farm place Seed time and harvest have not yet ceased in our land; but anyone who has observed our stack yards for many years, must deplore the falling off in workmanlike thrift and neatness which they used to exhibit. Badly made stacks in a farmyard are not only unsightly, but they tell the sad tale of careless husbandry, arising at the present time in great measure from the year to year system of farming. The temporary tenure of a farm has the worst possible effect on the farmer. It naturally begets the feeling that it is not worth while to maintain a high standard in anything. For this reason the land is in many cases starved, and by no means free from weeds and their roots, and only yields half the crops it grew of yore. Grass is rapidly taking the place of tilth, and whatever corn is grown is at harvest often thrown together by unskilled hands into the untidy stacks we so often see. "It is not worth while" - that is what the poor attenuated sheaf says as it is forked up - "I am of so little value." "It is not worth while," says

33

the ragged, ill-shaped, badly-made and badly-thatched stack; "I shall be thrashed out long before Christmas to pay the wages of those who have made me so badly."

That tall wiry looking man of seventy, how it makes his heart ache as be passes those same ill-made stacks. He was a notable 'man' at stacking in his day, and the farmer he worked for was fortunate in having him to build his ricks. It was worth while, then, to care both for the sheaf and for the stack. And our old friend firmly believes that even in these days of cheap corn it is worth while still. He loves to tell you of the days when the stack was, as it were, his castle, of which he was the complete master; how he used to build it up around him, with layer on layer of sheaves. With much gesticulation of his large and still powerful hands, he shows how, like the stones in a wall, the layers of sheaves were, as we may say, jointed together; and with much exertion he explains what he deems the real principle of stack making. All the way up the stack, in making every layer of sheaves, they are kept high or "full" in the centre, as though each layer was a sort of roof, so that all rain or damp entering at the top must run towards the sides. But while so careful of the internal structure of the stack, he is mindful of its outward form. To protect it from rain and drip from the well projecting eaves, the sides incline inwards at the bottom. It may look top heavy, but its weight keeps it as firm as a rock in the worst gale that blows. It was customary to trim the sides of the stacks by shearing them very evenly. In this way a neat look was given to the stack yard, and more than this, mice were thus in great measure excluded. The reaper now cuts the stalks of corn so unevenly that no attempt is made to trim the stacks, and the mice more easily get a lodgment.

Chapter VI

Harvest

A good harvest, and a good harvest season are two very different things. It is sad enough to have light crops, but it is far worse to have good crops giving a fair promise, ruined by the entire lack of reasonable weather for gathering them in.

In the year 1903 the corn grew thick on the ground, there were no bare places. Even on high, exposed land, it looked more than usually flourishing, and the colour of the blade did not pale in spite of a stormy summer. There was but little sunshine, and the corn ripened very slowly. It was evident that the harvest would be late, and that when ready it would not be quickly gathered in.

It was perhaps natural that our farmers should with some confidence expect the weather to change for the better. The doctrine of chances was in favour of a reaction. The rain and wind had had their turn, and something a little benign was reasonably hoped for.

The reapers and binders, repaired by the local blacksmith, were all ready for work, and some of the farmers, who could ill afford the outlay, had bought new machines this season.

Gangs of Irish labourers, tall, powerful, swarthy men, of somewhat unwieldy gait, hailing from Donegal and Connaught, tramped our roads, as they have done for many a year, in search of harvest work; but their number has become fewer each year, since the adoption of machinery instead of the sickles which these men invariably brought with them, bound with straw to preserve them from rust. They seem to know by instinct when the English farmer is in a difficulty. This year they went as usual from farm to farm offering their labour, which they well knew from the sight of the heavy crops would lie sorely needed, for it looked as if no machine could properly reap such fields.

No doubt these itinerant labourers are sometimes troublesome to deal with, and at some farms it is difficult to house and feed them; but this year, had they been employed, they could have saved, in a few fine days we had, a great part of the harvest now spoilt beyond recovery - a ten pound note spent in employing them would in many cases have saved several hundred pounds worth of property. Faith

35

is indeed of the very essence of human life and action, but we must beware of mistaking, as many do, fatalism for faith. It is consistent with faith for a man to use to the utmost all the powers and faculties he may possess.

It is quite true corn must have time to dry before it is carted and stacked, but there is generally opportunity, even in the worst harvest season, when it may be secured dry, if sufficient labour is available. Unfortunately the number of hands on our large farms is so much reduced, that, when a great pressure of work comes, with a heavy harvest and unfavourable stormy weather, the farm is quite unequal to the strain. Unless extra labour is employed at such a time it is hopeless to cope with the work, and the crops must take their chance. To those who know what farming has been in the past, it is a sad sight to see the sheaves, tossed from the machines all over a thirty acre field, and left lying on the ground, to the mercy of the weather, for want of hands to set up the stooks. This is bad enough in good weather, but it is fatal in a wet season. The sheaves tied by the machine with cord are much more difficult to dry than those bound by hand with straw bands.

It is far too late in the day to say a word against the use of machinery in farming, but when machinery is allowed to lead to carelessness, instead of thrift, there is a great danger to be guarded against.

If corn is worth sowing and reaping it is worth saving. It has an intrinsic value of its own as a precious gift to man, apart from its mere commercial price Its true value was best shown in the old days when the shearer swept it together with his sickle, gathered it to his bosom, and bound it into the sheaf, a precious burden for human arms to lift.

The sickle is now a thing of the past. It is doubtful whether many men of our countryside know how to use it. The scythe is generally employed for opening up a passage for the reaping machine in the fields.

The thing that seems to strike the old hands most, as they look on at modern methods of farming, is indifference to the crop after it is grown. They do not find fault with labour saving machinery, for they have a painful recollection of their past toils when all farm work was hand labour. To the enquiry "You know all about shearing?" an old hind of eighty-five replies, "Ah, that I do, your back was that sair after ten hours at it, that you had to 'scraffle' on the ground, before you could lift yourself up."

But what these old hands think, rightly or wrongly, is, that, with machinery, has come some degree of carelessness; and that the fields in which they once toiled so hard yield fewer bushels to the acre than they remember. They will name a field which grew wheat enough to pay the rent of the whole farm, and a large rent too, double to what it pays the landlord now. This no doubt is an exaggeration, but there is some truth in it.

There is one thing that they forget, and that is that in their young days wheat was a thing of value, but now its price is so low that it does not pay to grow it, and it has in our district almost gone out of cultivation. If the clergyman of the parish can get a sheaf of wheat to decorate his church for the harvest festival he is fortunate.

That deep interest which dependence on hand labour for harvest work created cannot be expected to return: but it was a wonderful thing in its day, and the memory of it is very strong in the aged labourers who dearly love to talk about it; indeed it seems to give some of them a fresh lease of life, to find a friend who likes to hear of the old ways of tillage, and the old life of the field worker.

An aged villager who has known the country and its ways for four score years and more, tells me a fact about reaping hooks which if known to a few, will soon be quite forgotten. They had fine teeth, like a saw, and finer than the teeth in a rat trap. The "teethed hewk", as it was called, was indeed a very delicate instrument. It was shaped like the more modern sickle but the blade was very narrow throughout the whole length of its curve. This was the ancient reaping hook, which had not changed its form for centuries. There is not one to be found in the parish now; but many an old man and woman can tell you how they used it when they were young, how hard it was to learn its use, and how when the knack of it was caught, it did better work than the sickle that came after it.

It was the use of the "teethed hewk" that was called hand shearing," because it was necessary for the left hand to grasp the wheat stalks, that they might offer sufficient resistance to the saw edge of the hook, brought around them by a deft movement of the right hand. The "teethed hewk" seems to have seldom needed sharpening, and if so, it must have been made of steel of excellent quality. It could only cut as much as the left hand could grasp or "roll" together at one time, but, in this way, it cut more thoroughly, and longer straw, leaving the stubble short and clean. For these reasons, many farmers continued the use of the "teethed hewk" after the smooth edged sickle was introduced. It may seem strange that, what is to us so old fashioned an implement as the sickle, should have been received at its first introduction with some of the same kind of prejudice and reluctance as that with which modern machinery was at first regarded; but so it was.

The knife of the modern reaping machine, a horizontal bar from which teeth project, is a remarkable instance of the permanence of old principles even where there seems to be the greatest change. What could seem less like the reaping hook than the present day reaper with its whirling fans, and yet the long knife which cuts the corn has a saw edge like the old teethed hook, but, of course, with much larger teeth. The first reaping machine had knives with a smooth edge, following the principle of the sickle, but afterwards an edge with large teeth was found necessary.

The sickle, of course, could cut more corn at a time with a single sweep of the right arm; a movement which was called "striking" in contradistinction to hand shearing. The left arm was free to gather the stalks after they were cut, and an armful instead of a handful was set down for the bindster.

It is said that a practised hand, brought up to use the teethed hook, could cut quite as much corn, and as quickly, as a shearer using the sickle. There was a knack of gathering the corn in the hand which was called "rolling", and which when acquired enabled a large bunch to be cut with the teethed hook very quickly. It was easier to be rash and hasty with the sickle, and the cutting could not be so close; besides it was thought that the time lost in sharpening the sickle made it doubtful which hook cut most in a given time.

"I gloried in shearing" said an old friend to me in talking of these things. He went on to tell me that once in the harvest field he sharpened his teethed "hewk" so that the edge became quite smooth like a sickle, and he began to sweep down the corn with it enjoying the freedom he found in using it in this new way. The steward came up, and, surprised at his method of reaping asked what it meant. My friend told him that it was indeed the teethed "hewk" he was using. The steward remarked "It must be a good one, then."

Mrs. Burns, fifty years ago sheared with teethed hewk for Wm.

Jobson, farmer of Turvelaws, near Wooler, who would not allow the sickle to be used, and his rule was that there should be three good handfuls to a sheaf. Even after the sickle came into use for wheat and oats, barley was still cut by hand shearing whether with teethed hook or sickle ; the left hand being used to hold the corn while being cut. Barley straw being weaker than that of wheat, would not so well stand against the stroke of the sickle.

Of course the teethed hewk did not cut so wide a space at a time as the sickle, and this is why the old rigs were much narrower than the later ones : the width cut by each worker being less, more workers were required in the space. The old rigs or divisions of the field were five yards wide. The more modern division contained two of these and were ten yards wide and called the "bandwin."

There were never less than three shearers in a rank on the "bandwin," sometimes there were four, two being children in that case, and counting as one grown person. Between the shearers on one rig and those on the next, there was a man called "bindster," who used to bind the sheaves for both rigs, and sharpen the sickles for the women shearers.

The bandwin really means the breadth of corn which furnished sheaves sufficient for one man's labour to bind; and it was the general rule for one bindster to follow four shearers, and bind the handfuls they laid down.

The bindster, who followed the shearers, was supplied with bands by one of the women, who, as she reaped, would every now and then make a band, and throw it down for him. The band was quickly made, by giving the handful of corn a double twist near the head; and woe to the woman who only made one twist, and supplied "slipped" bands. The band, when made, was laid down across the rig, and upon it the handfuls of two shearers was laid. All was thus in order for the bindster, as he came on behind. A man named Robert Bone used to come out of Scotland and do harvest work. He was a man of great strength. He would sometimes say to the woman working beside him, "You just make bands," and he then sheared the whole rig, keeping in line with the rest of the workers.

The following story of the harvest field was related by an old worker, of her mother's great grandmother.

A farmer had all his shearers allotted for the day to reap a field, when a wayfaring man came up to him and asked for work. The farmer was fully supplied with hands, and told the man so, but asked him to have some breakfast, which he accepted. He thanked the farmer for his kindness, and was walking away, when the farmer called him back. "I have reconsidered the matter," he said, "and as there is some air blowing, I will take one of my hands off, and set him to lift the corn where it is down, and I will give you some shearing to do. But what wage do you expect?" "Well, sir," said the stranger, "I will take the wages of two women." "That is out of the question," said the master "I do not think so," said the man," "but if you find that I do the work of two women, will you give me the money I ask?" "That I will do," said the farmer. So the work began, but not without strong objection from the women shearers, two of whom had to work in line with him on the same rig. They soon found still more cause for complaint, for their strange fellow worker laboured with such tremendous energy and quickness, that they found it a terrible strain to keep up with him. Yet it was a point of honour not to be outstripped. All the reapers on the other rigs were keenly alive to the situation, and the race for the end of the rig became general all along the line. It was on the second rig of the field that the stranger and the two women were reaping, and so rapid was their progress that they reached the end and got half way down the next rig, before the other reapers had only got to the top. The man now saw that the two women were sore distressed in the contest which they carried on out of a mixture of spite and determination not to be beaten in the race, so he said to them,"now if you like to go easy, I will slacken my pace, but if you will not I am quite ready to continue the contest." Tradition does not say whether they consented, but the mysterious shearer worked for the farmer to the end of that harvest and promised to come in future years, but was never seen again. So calmly and rapidly did he work, that while reaping he also threw aside every now and then a twisted band to the bindster for binding the sheaves.

The shearer worked along the rigs generally from west to east. The leading rig was the one to the left and the chief man there, was the leader, and used to get very angry if anyone else in the line got ahead of him in reaping. It was very often a race which set of shearers should outstep the other. This emulation in the harvest field was called "kemping" and when it took place, as it too often did, the field was said to be "on the kemp." The word is evidently akin to the German "kampfen," combat, struggle, strive.

There is no scene of industry in our countryside at all approaching in animation and picturesque effect to the shearing of a large field of wheat sixty years ago. There are, say, twenty rigs each ten yards wide. The farmer's whole force is present, and many hired hands besides. The workers in a long line from end to end of the field, four on each rig, and a man to bind; making in all one hundred hands, are drawn up like a company in open order, as if to advance against an enemy. At first it looks a peaceful contest enough, the golden heads of corn make neither attack nor defence, but they fall as the reapers evenly advance, and the width of stubble gradually but surely widens. It is a wonderful scene of well organized labour, and harmony and good nature reign throughout the field. But some young man, fond of a joke, has cast a firebrand of mischief among the workers. He has suggested to the shearers at the end of the line furthest from where he works, that the women at his rig intend to run them hard, and outstrip them in the work; and coming back to his own place, tells the women for whom he binds, that those at the other end are preparing to outdo them. Angry and suspicious looks are quickly cast across the field, and in a few moments the real battle has begun. All the shearers redouble their labour, the whole field is "on the kemp;" and the line becomes irregular, on some rigs the workers gain rapidly, making quite a lane into the corn; some are even; some advance and then fall back. The strife is fast and furious, angry passions are aroused, especially among the women. The sickle is used recklessly, and the corn badly cut. The steward cries out to his people to stop the foolish strife, but they pay no heed; he knows too well that he is helpless, for does he not remember how on one occasion, Mabon, the Amazon of the field, when he planted his stick to arrest her furious shearing, cut it in two with a sweep of her sickle, and threatened to do the same with him unless he stood out of her road.

Some farmers might think it an advantage for the workers to redouble their exertions at no extra cost to themselves, but not the thrifty ones, for the work was badly done and much corn was left on the ground. Some farmers would stand near their shearers and threaten to thrash them when they saw signs of "kemping." Curiously enough, the harvest time is said to have been the only time our people fell out, and certainly, from all accounts, "kemping"

41

aroused the most angry feelings among them. The usual cause of the strife was connected with the furrow (1) or depression, between two rigs; this was the border line between two sets of shearers. It was the duty of the shearer on the right of each rig to cut the corn in the furrow or "slack" between that rig and the next. Any neglect in clearing the furrow threw more work on the neighbouring shearer. No corn must be left standing, or the hands on both rigs would be blamed by the master, who was sure to detect the fault.

As the old hands constantly tell you, "they was more partic'lar with the corn in them days," and this care was shown in every process of its cultivation and in gathering, from the time it was sown as bare grain, to the time it became bare grain again on the barn floor. This care was especially shown in setting up, or stooking, the sheaves in the field. The sheaves in the stook were generally ten in number leaning against one another. The angle at which they were sloped was considered a matter of great importance. It was imperative that it should be an acute angle, so that the rain might run off easily, as in the case of the roofs of ancient houses, which are invariably high-pitched. So particular were the farmers, that, if one ear of corn was seen lying the wrong way in the sheaf before binding, it had to be taken out and laid the proper way. If any ears rose above the level of the rest, at the top of the stook, they were ordered to be pulled out and put into a new sheaf. The stook had to be made so that you could look through it from end to end, and also across between the sheaves from side to side, so that the air might go freely through or "wise in," as the people have it.

In order to obtain as much sunshine in the day as possible, to dry the sheaves after they were set up, the stooks were so placed that the ends pointed north-east and south-west. They then got the morning sun on the south-east side, the midday sun on both sides, and the afternoon sun on the north-west side ; and as the Cheviot Hills are to the south-west of us, the rule on all our farms was to build the stook with one end towards the Cheviot, or to be more exact, towards the small lump or hillock on the west end of Cheviot. This by long usage was the rule, and the farmers used to insist upon its

(1) This is the reason given by the people for these contests, but most likely "kemping" arose in the first place from the very ancient strife amongst the reapers to cut down the last sheaf of the harvest.

observance. With the depreciation in the value of corn this extreme care in what was considered in important point, is unknown, and the stooks are placed with little method.

There was a plan of saving corn in showery weather which was found very useful. It was adopted sometimes when the corn was cut in a somewhat wet state. It was called "gatening" or more correctly "gaiting." Instead of the bindster binding up the sheaf, the shearer would herself bind it very lightly, not round the middle but just below the ears. She would then stand each sheaf firmly on the field, spreading out the stalks to support it. The sheaves would be left thus standing separately, and would dry better than in any other way.

Stooks of wheat sometimes contained as many as fourteen sheaves, six on each side, and two above to form a sort of thatched roof. It was worth while in bad weather to risk the damage of the two sheaves above, if the twelve below were saved. This process was called "hooding." It was often used in fields with woods adjoining them, to protect the grain from the ravages of rooks. To keep the sample fair, barley was always hooded.

In France and Germany "hooding" the stooks is very general. There was also a way of arranging four sheaves to form a small stook. This plan allowed the air to get in at the corners. It was called "willow draggling," which appears to be a Scotch expression, but the practice was in general use on the English Border. "Willow draggling" was much used in harvesting beans.

The round stacks of corn in our North-country farm yards are not perhaps so neatly trimmed as the large oblong stack of the South of England, but they are in shape and size quite suited to the climate. It is no small part of the farmer's anxiety that a "hard wind" should blow through and between his stacks, as they stand rank after rank within the low walls of his farm yard. How often one has heard the wish expressed for that hard wind to blow after the corn is cut. It matters not which "airt" it blows from, as long as it is hard, cold, and penetrating. It is better than sunshine. It keeps the corn from sprouting as it stands in the stook, and it prevents it heating in the stack, and prepares it for the thrasher. Sad to say this season, 1903, the hard wind came too soon. Just when the grain was ripening and on the eve of being cut, a fierce strong gale blew from the west. This was the first disaster of our harvest. A "shake," is the great dread of the farmer, and a "shake" it was indeed. It took the heart out of many a well-to-do man, when in a few hours the hope of his toil was gone, and he could roughly estimate his loss at several hundred pounds. Whole fields of barley in exposed places were stripped of their beard and grain, and the bare stalks left standing. The oats, more yielding, held up white empty grain cases to the light. A "shake " like this is a disaster indeed, and for sheer unavoidable destruction must be classed with the earthquake, and the volcanic eruption, as far as property is concerned. It must be taken, however, as one of the risks of farming.

And the same must be said of the phenomenal rains which followed. There were many districts in which a large acreage of corn was still unharvested although Hallowe'en was past. In many upland exposed places, the wet sunless weather prevented the corn from ripening, and when cut incessant rain ensued.

Our harvest in 1904 was very much better than that of the previous year. The perfect summer led one to expect it would be so. All vegetation seemed to grow vigorously, in the growing time, and to develop properly without drawbacks. When the harvest actually set in without any of the dreaded shaking wind, and little if any of the corn laid by storm and rain, the sense or satisfaction was very great.

It is an unusual thing for our farmers and labourers to express this satisfaction; our people seem to have a superstitious dread of praising anything, but this year all freely admitted that the harvest was an excellent one. One might of course judge that it was so, from the stack yards being so full that many ricks are seen in adjoining fields. But this is not the surest evidence. It is the farmer and the farm servant who really know the truth about the harvest. It is not until the threshing that the whole truth is known. For the straw may be out of all proportion to the grain, and on the other hand, a stack may thresh out well, but it may not mean many bushels to the acre.

It is not often in the course of a lifetime you hear from the worker such expressions as these : "The best harvest for twenty-five years." "The best in a' my time." "Aye, the farmer has nothing to complain of this season." "Tis been a profitable harvest, 'twas all standing corn and none to lift."

And no Irishmen was employed, they was na' needed.

Chapter VII

Harvest Customs

Among harvest customs which have died out in our district, but which live in the memory of our people, the most curious and probably the most primitive is that of the "kirn dolly" (1).

This was made not of the first fruits of the harvest, but of the very last sheaf, of the last field cut, upon the farm. There was much rivalry among the shearers to obtain this last "grip," as it was termed, and to cut it. This sheaf was nicely rounded by the workers, and fully dressed with a skirt, and ribbons round the neck, to represent a young girl. It was raised aloft upon a fork, and carried about the field with dancing and singing to the strains of the local fiddler, his fiddle being decorated with coloured ribbons like the pipes of the Scotch pipers. It was ultimately carried in procession to the farmyard, where, as the people say, the farmer showed hospitality.

There was also the procession of the last load, after the rest of the harvest was all carried. One of the women workers was mounted on the top of the load, which was accompanied by all the harvesters, from the field to the front door of the farm house, with music and singing. Here the farmer's wife appeared, and was expected to take the whip and drive the horse and cart to the stackyard. This done, she selected a small bunch of wheat ears from the cart, and returned to the house, having provided food and drink for the hands. In a case where she showed no inclination to show hospitality, the hands would, as a penalty, make it difficult for her to drive the horse.

The antiquary will no doubt be able to throw some light upon these curious customs, which are probably practised in some such form in many parts of the world. They are evidently survivals of ancient rites connected with the worship of the Corn Spirit, and expressive of thankfulness for the fruits of the earth in their season. The term "kirn" is now only applied to the harvest home dance given by the farmer to the hands after the corn is all led and comfortably stacked for the winter. The "kirn dolly" used to be kept until the kirn dance, and was then again exhibited in the barn where the dance took place.

At the conclusion of the shearing and in connection with the kirn

45

dolly custom, a practical joke was played on the farmer if he dared to show himself in the field, and this he took good care as a rule not to do. It was called "putting up the master." (2)

If the farmer by any mischance made his appearance, it was the custom for the hands, chiefly the women workers, to set on him, pull him off his horse, and "grip" him, and toss him in the air, not only once, but three or four times, catching him as he fell.

Once a farmer had as his visitor a friend from London, who, as may be supposed, knew nothing of this custom. He took him into the field, having previously arranged with his people that they should "put him up." The farmer, walking in amongst them with his friend, gave them as a signal a quiet nod over his shoulder. They at first hesitated to do his bidding, thinking it too bad to take a stranger by surprise in so rough a manner, but another nod from their master meaning, "put him up," was taken as a command, and the poor man, who was somewhat stout, was suddenly "gripped" by a number of strong hands and tossed up and down, again and again, crying in terror, "What's the matter? Thompson, Thompson, come here! What's all this? What have I done? Oh take care of my watch," etc., until, panting and trembling, he was again placed on his feet. It was, naturally, some time before his anger was appeased, and before he could receive with good grace the explanation of his friend that it was an old harvest custom (3).

Many a farmer now living on the Borders has undergone this sort of penance. Like the "barring out" of the school-master, it was a good natured way of showing that old scores, if there were any, could be paid off, even by the women workers. It says a great deal for the strength, nerve and dexterity of the harvest maidens of those days, that the farmer was always safely caught after his tossing, and suffered no harm.

Of course the flail disappeared long ago, probably sooner from our district than many parts of England, but it is often spoken of by our aged folk. There is still a building in our village, now a joiner's shop, which was allowed to be the thrashing floor of the villagers. The old people used to gather at the open barn doors, and gossip about past and present threshers, their strength and endurance, and how many bushels to the acre the corn was yielding. The children would eagerly watch the fall of the flails with their measured beat, and admire the goodly heap of yellow grain, and the floor polished with the labour and the constant sweeping aside of the corn. As there were champion shearers, so there were threshers who were known for their special prowess in wielding the flail, and who used to go from farm to farm to ply their calling. Some of the best of these men continued their use of the flail for some time after threshing machines were generally used.

Threshing machines were first adopted in Northumberland about 1763 (4). The idea was taken from the flax mill used in swingling flax. Men used to travel about with these swingling machines, visiting the farm places where flax was grown and spun for household use. At first the motive power for the thresher was supplied by a man working a treadle; this gave place to water power, which is still used on some of our farms. It is only of late years that the round roof which used to shelter the horse, which worked some of the threshers, has disappeared from our farm yards, though long ago disused. The travelling or fixed steam engine now does all this work which naturally takes the place of other work in bad winter weather. One of the first threshing machines used in the county was put up at the farm of East Flodden by a Mr. Oxley.

It may be a fitting close to this chapter on harvest matters to insert the following songs taken down from the lips of an aged parishioner. His father, he says, was a great singer. He had a good store of songs, some of which had come down to him by word of mouth, and others were ballads such as were sold on sheets at country fairs, or patriotic songs about Nelson and Waterloo, as sung by strolling sailors and soldiers returned from the wars, and appealing for charity as the unemployed heroes of their country.

The two harvest songs are certainly old. The first is advice from a young man to his sweetheart who wishes to work with him, but who, he thinks, is not suited to the rough work of shearing

The shearin's not for you, Bonnie Peggy, O,
The shearin's not for you, Bonnie Peggy, O,
The shearin's not for you'
It takes wit and method, too,
And strength to carry't through, Bonnie Peggy, O.
Dres't in your corset stays, Bonnie Peggy, O,
Dres't in your corset stays, Bonnie Peggy, O,
Dres't in your corset stays,

47

Whilst the sunbeams on ye blaze,
No mair need to strip your claithes, Bonnie Peggy, O.
Spread yourself below, Bonnie Peggy, O,
Spread yourself below, Bonnie Peggy, O,
Spread yourself below,
Let the air about ye blow,
And keep your elbow low, (5) Bonnie Peggy, O.
Follow to your hook, Bonnie Peggy, O.
Follow to your hook, Bonnie Peggy, O.
Follow to your hook,
And keep a sharp look oot
That you'r up with other folk, Bonnie Peggy, O.
The rule's correct and plain, Bonnie Peggy, O,
The rule's correct and plain, Bonnie Peggy, O,
The rule's correct and plain,
But advice is all in vain, (6)
Where strength and spirits gain, Bonnie Peggy, O.

The other song, evidently brought across the Border from Scotland, is an invitation from a gallant young shearer to his sweetheart to work with him:-

Bonnie lassie wilt thou gang, (7)
And shear wi' me this hale day lang?
And love will cheer us as we gang,
    To join yon hand o' shearers.
The neighbours they do us envy,
They say there's love 'twixt you and I,
But carelessly we'll pass them by,
    As we go to the shearing.
The thristles they stan' stewt and strong,
For fear your milk white hand should wrong,
I'll take my sledge and mow them down,
    When we are at the shearing.
And when the shearing is a' done
We will have a rantin' kirn,
And in some cosy neuk we'll make but little din,
    And forget a' the toils o' the shearing.

48

(1) Frazer has collected much evidence to show that a harvest custom of the same sort prevails in many countries, and his theory that the last sheaf of the harvest is believed to embody the Corn Spirit, is well supported. - Golden Bough, vol. II, chap iii.

(2) Frazer shows that this rough handling of the farmer at the end of harvest is as primitive and widespread as any other folklore custom. "In the Canton of Putanges in Normandy, the custom of tying up the owner of the land in the last sheaf of wheat is still practised," or, at least, was still practised some thirteen or fourteen years ago (written in 1890). The task falls to the women alone. They throw themselves upon the proprietor, seize him by the arms, the legs, and the body, throw him to the ground and stretch him upon the last sheaf. Then a pretence is made of binding him, and the conditions to be observed at the harvest supper are dictated to him. When he has accepted them, he is released, and allowed to get up. - Golden Bough, vol. III, p. 232.

(3) The idea seems to be that the proprietor, like the last sheaf, is an embodiment of the Corn Spirit and is to be reaped and bound and handled as the sheaf is. And comparative folk-lore leads to the belief that in our old custom of putting up the farmer or the man who has cut the last sheaf we have traces of the practice of human sacrifices which in the ancient world and among rude races in more recent times have been offered to promote the fertility of the earth. - Golden Bough vol. II., chap. iii.

(4) Bailey and Culley's *General View of the Agriculture of Northumberland*, 1797.

(5) A cardinal point in shearing.

(6) This refers to the exciting competition between the shearers called "kemping".

(7) Learnt more than seventy years ago and very old then.

CHAPTER VIII.

The Back End.

In the language of our people, the "back end" of the year has fully come. The aspect of the wide landscape, across the flat valley to the opposite hill, is slowly but surely changing. Each week you see less of the stubble and grass, and more of the plough land. The colour is not so cheerful, and it does not reflect the transient bands of sunlight so well, but it is deep and rich in tone, and has more of purple than of brown or red. It is a great stretch of country; there are portions of several estates and many farms in view. The fields are large, some of them forty acres in extent . If they were smaller they would look too much like a map, and spoil the landscape. As it is, the plough-ing harmonizes the view and brings it nearer to the colour of the moorland of the Cheviots which forms the background. As we see the ploughman thus "overtaking the reaper," there is a mingled feeling of regret and hope. There is no standing still in the labour of the fields. The plough is the emblem of progress. As soon as the harvest is off the land, the plough is in the furrow; but as the soil is cut by the coulter, and turned gently over from the breast of the plough-share, we feel that the summer garb of nature is put off and buried, and her winter dress put on. Slowly but surely the sombre colour of a thousand well made furrows spreads from farm to farm, over the scene. The hedgerows, now browned with autumn, become less visible, and the only green spaces that will soon be left are the turnips which the sheep are already devouring, and the dear old grass fields, which, like the ancient church of the village, are more valued the older they become. Happy is the farmer who has, near his homestead, a wide stretch of this permanent pasture. It has never felt the plough-share for centuries, unless perhaps in the time of the French wars, when wheat meant gold, and every available acre was sown with it.

But you cannot look day by day upon the changing landscape of October without having in mind the agency which causes the change. In this first process of agriculture, the ploughing of the land, the primitive method still holds good. Each one of the million furrows that make up the ever increasing breadth of tilth, is set up by the skill of the man whose hand controls, and whose eye directs, the plough. It is hard work you will say, plodding all day long, and every day for months in the wettest and most unpleasant season of the year.

How monotonous such labour, you may think. But do not judge of another's work from your own point of view. Ask the ploughman himself, and what will he tell you? He will smile at your sympathy, and tell you that his work is the lightest labour of any on the farm. Of course, there are awkward hands that never learn the knack and mystery of the work and these, no doubt, do find it hard; but not so the skilled ploughman, who, with a light hand on the stilts, and in perfect sympathy with his clever horses, goes forward, "smooring along," setting "her," the land, well up, and making a fine "whole " but narrow furrow that rejoices his heart by its excellence.   As, borne up by the "stilts," his feet move easily along the deep but level path made by the sole of the plough, he thinks of the saying of his father, who was an adept in the same calling: "If you was fairly oot and yokéd the sairest of our work would be o'er." I do not say that the ploughman's work is light, but that it is lighter than most other occupations of the kind, and not nearly so severe as it would seem to the ordinary spectator. The fine well trained horses supply the motive power, and are wonderfully clever. The horse on the right that goes in the furrow can never be diverted from it.

It is impossible for the ploughman to feel dull. He has far too much to see to. From the time that the field is set out, and the first straight furrow is drawn from mark to mark, there is no looking back. It is forward work all the time; the horses know well how to turn at the head-rig, but they often need a gentle word of restraint or encouragement. It is far from dull if there are several teams at work in the same field; and even if the hind, as he ploughs, hears no other human voice but his own, hundreds of white gulls from the Farne Islands bear him company, every now and then rising into the air with whirring wings, and then, as the plough advances, gently alighting to find their food in the freshly turned soil.   The ploughman is, as a rule, a cheery being. His work may look monotonous, but there is far more science in his trade than other people think. In the days of his fathers, agriculture was a fine art, and the highest excellence was aimed at. He had been told that "a plough is the same as a fiddle, it has to be 'kept in tune.' " He knows that the future crop greatly depends upon the excellence of his work. The furrow must be made fit to receive into its bosom first the frost and moisture of winter, and then the seed in spring. What outsider would understand the importance of setting up the ridge that its "shoulder " should be so placed that after the seed falls into the furrow, the harrow driven across it should more effectually cover it in with soil, and so protect it in its growth, and establish it against storm and stress of weather.

The "whole furrow," that is the continuous unbroken ridge set up by the plough-share, is the ploughman's delight and pride, and so he sets his face against the wheeled plough which has been in use for some years. It has had a fair trial, but is now lying discarded. It breaks up the surface of the land and does not go deep enough. The usual English plough makes a "whole furrow" without breaking it up, thus allowing rain in autumn and winter to get down at once into the land between one furrow and another. The frost then comes and bursts the soil and pulverizes it naturally. Nothing encourages the growth of thistles so much as the breaking up of the furrow, and a field of thistles is a terrible blot on the country side.

The evolution of the plough would be a fascinating subject to pursue, but if we follow its history from its most ancient to its most modern form, it remains, in principle and general aspect, the same all the world over. Like the keel of a ship which ploughs the wave, and the bit in the horse's mouth, it takes its form from the work it has always had to do, in association and direct contact with Nature, and so has always remained the same. It is the soil that has formed the plough, and it is the soil that will always regulate its shape, improve it as you will. Its framework is now of iron; many of us remember when it was of wood, and the "irons "of the plough meant its "sock " or point in front, its coulter, or, as we say it, "couter," the vertical blade that cuts the soil, and its "share" that shears and throws over the furrow from its curved and polished "breast." The old wood framed ploughs look well in a painting of rustic life, and they did good work in their long day, but light ironwork is more durable, and better to handle, and it supports the plough irons as well as wood. There is a village not far away, which was considered a "terrible hole" in the old days, for rough conduct. At one farm there, when the men took out the wooden ploughs in the morning, they all went to pieces, the beam of each plough having been sawn nearly through in the night.

An old man of Yetholm used to tell our blacksmith, that, in his younger days, he knew a young man who attended ploughing matches and took all the first prizes. He used to bring the different parts of his wooden plough, and its irons, in a bag, and put them together in the field where the contest was to take place.

Although the old grass fields in the landscape remain green in the midst of the dark plough land, many of them tell a story of the plough which goes back to a very remote time. Their surface is not even, but undulating, like the sand of the sea shore, after the tide has passed over and receded from it. These ridges are about five yards wide, on an average, with a deep slack between them. Their great peculiarity is that they are rarely straight, but curved, and if the field is large they have a double curve and are serpentine or "twisty," as our people express it. Of their age it is hard to judge, but they are here called "lang syne rigs." Who knows but that they were formed by Saxon ploughmen or by those who cultivated our hill slopes with terraced balks in still earlier times! They were evidently made before the land was enclosed, as the direction of the rigs bear no relation to the modern dykes. When we look out upon these fine sweeping curves, and walk across their undulating surface, we feel quite sure that the acknowledged value of old grass has here preserved for us, and generally near the homesteads, a feature of great antiquity.

Very curious are some of the reasons given by our people to account for the curvature of these rigs. There is no doubt that oxen drew the ploughs that first formed them, and that they were ploughed by oxen until they were left exactly as we now see them. But that the rigs were made in parallel curves, to ease the oxen on the hill side, as a tired man in ascending a bank, goes not straight upwards but from side to side, is incredible, for oxen trained to plough are very strong; besides, these rigs occur on comparatively level ground in some places. Another theory is that it was the tendency of the old plough to swerve to the left, that this accounts for the single curve, and that the second curve of the serpentine form arose from the effort of the goad's-man to turn the cattle to the right. This is quite untenable, for the rigs are not the result of chance and the caprice of the plough or the oxen, but are clearly planned to take the form they do, as they are generally of even width and parallel.

It has also been said that the curve resulted from the fact that the cattle worked in single file, sometimes to the number of six, and that therefore it was necessary to make a broad sweep round, as a sudden turn at the end of the rig would have been impossible. This does seem a probable theory, for the ancient "sheths," or portions of land sometimes had boundaries, and cattle working in single file, say, to the number of six, unless they crossed the boundary at the beginning and end of each furrow, would need to draw the plough in a wide curve. But it is doubtful whether the oxen often worked in single file. An inhabitant tells me that he understood that the reason the ancient ox rigs went in a curved or sinuous form was to prevent the rainfall draining off too suddenly from the land, and so carrying away the soil with it, as it would have done if these high rigs had been straight. This reason would seem probable if it were found that the rigs always ran with the general slope of the ground.

As far as the height of these rigs is concerned, one explanation of our people is that they were so made to increase the superficial area of a given quantity of land. It is evident that land made undulating by artificial means has a greater surface than the same land when the surface was even. It is clear that the surface is larger, and in a grass field of this kind more grass can be grown, but it is a debatable question whether more corn could be grown. A retired farmer assures me that his people once had a field, which, when they entered upon the farm, was twelve acres in extent, but that by "gathering" the land into high ridges, in imitation of the old rigs, they so increased the surface that there was, when they left the farm, a gain of one acre within the same boundaries.

The only general theory that will reasonably account for the curvature as well as the height of the rigs is the drainage of the land. It has been suggested to me, by a friend who has given much attention to such enquiries, that there seems to be a striking analogy between those high curved rigs, and the condition of land that has been flooded with water, and then drained by natural means. And it is quite true that, viewing our valley as a whole, and having in mind the large fields where these rigs occur, whether on the hill sides, or on the more level land near the river bank, it would be easy to imagine that these effects were left on the surface of the land by the natural action of the pre-historic lake as it gradually subsided and dwindled until it became the sluggish Till. But this analogy, striking as it is, is only suggested to point to the apparent imitation of the processes of Nature in artificial drainage of the land in early times. Whether we find them on the low lying land or the hill slopes it is clear that the high rigs heaped up by the plough by a process called "gathering" were so made to throw the water off into the "slack" between them. But it is not so obvious that the curvature of the rigs in their course was designed for the same purpose, as it may have been. Large spaces of land are never uniformly level or of uniform slope, even the best made tennis lawn will soon have its depressions, however slight. It is possible that the rigs were made curved, and sometimes serpentine in their course, to suit the lie of the land, just as in our valley the river never runs straight, but makes a hundred curious curves and windings in its course towards the Tweed. It is true this does not prove the case, because the rigs are, as a rule, parallel. And so some people have fallen back on what, I hear, is an old superstition that "water will never run straight" and they give that as the reason for the peculiar course of the rigs which were made, as it were, to humour the water (1).

But after all, superstition has ever been one of the strongest motives to human action, and I will add to all the reasons I have given for the twisted form of the high rigs the tradition I have heard from two persons in this district. It is that our Saxon forefathers did not dare to plough straight because it was their belief that, if they did, the fairies would shoot their cattle. This certainly would account for the double curve of the rigs in large fields. The single curve, of course, could not be continuous, and if superstition prevented the furrow going straight, after the first curve was made, the only way was to reverse the curve and make the whole furrow serpentine.

It seems possible that this solution may be the right one. This curious tradition is in itself most interesting, and if correct it points to the great age of these twisted rigs. One is reminded by it of the tradition that the streets of our ancient towns and villages were built in zig-zag fashion, to prevent a real enemy from shooting their arrows so as to rake the streets from end to end. In his *Traffics and Discoveries*, Kipling has a poem called "The King's Task," in which he describes the enduring marks made by Saxon rule in England. The poem concludes with the four following lines:-

"Behind the feet of the Legions and before the Northman's
    fire,
Rudely but greatly begat they the body of state and of shire,
Rudely but greatly they laboured, and their labour stands
    till now,
If we trace on our ancient headlands the twist of their eight-
    ox plough."

It is a peculiar feature of these ancient rigs that the top soil is of
the same thickness in the depression between them as on the higher
parts of them. This is somewhat strange because the continual
gathering up of the soil into the high ridges would naturally have
the effect of thinning the soil in the lower parts between them. But
most probably, in the course of time, the rank vegetation in the
slack, which carried off the water from the ridges, would form a soil
of itself quite as thick as that on the more elevated parts.

The late Sir Jacob Wilson in conversation, when referring to soil
on these old fields, told me that great injury had been done to the
land by levelling these rigs to suit modern methods of farming, and
for this reason:- The reduction of the height of the rigs had laid
bare the subsoil and made barren strips.

Farm labourers have told me how their masters held out against
ploughing out the old rigs. They kept them as long as they could in
the same form. But the change was inevitable when the reaping
machine came into use. Machinery tends to bring everything to a
dead level. The reaper must have a broad and even track. Speaking
of the time when first many of the old rigs were levelled, an aged
farm worker exclaimed to me, "Oh, what a corn there was growed
where the slack used to be," and no doubt there was an equally poor
crop where the rig used to be. There are now none more ready to
see the advantage of machinery in agriculture than the field worker,
because it has so greatly lightened the labour but ask his candid
opinion of the present condition of the land, and he will tell you, in
his own way of speaking, that "it is sixty years back'" that it would
take many years to get the land in a condition to grow wheat, that
the modern system of land drainage is worn out, and that we may
have to go back to the old rigs yet. Of course this will be called
random talk, but it comes from the people who are part and parcel
of the fields, and in whom all the traditions of farming are, as it

were, inborn. When an old hind tells you "the land is all going back," "no manure is put into it," "the farmer don't want to have the corn grow strong because then the reapers would not cut it," you may not believe it at all, but you cannot help feeling that there is truth in it.

It is extraordinary how easily primitive things form an attractive picture. You pass along a straight familiar road, leading from one village to another. It is a winter afternoon, the sun is getting low in the west. It is not a spot at which you generally turn to view the landscape. There are distant hills, and the sky is pale in colour but brilliant. There is a picture all the same which arrests your attention. It is the outline and form of horses, men and ploughs, in line, dark against the sky. The picture moves slowly along the crest of the field, and you pass on your way, glad to feel that no ungraceful noisy machine has yet supplanted the plough, which the ingenuity of man finds it hard to improve in any essential particular.

But ploughing has its traditions in our country side, and to those who know them, the picture against the afternoon sky undergoes in the mind's eye a marked change. The rugged forms of oxen take the place of horses, and instead of the thin stilts of the iron plough, you see the outward sweep of its rough wooden handles, which you know are glossy with use and contact with the human hand. There are living in our district several persons who have traditions of the use of oxen both for ploughing and draft in Glendale, and also on the Scottish border. One who is eighty-five tells me that his father, when a lad, was goadsman to oxen-ploughing on a farm at Milfield. A steward of one of our large farms says that his father used to see ploughing by oxen, and that they sometimes walked in single file, one before the other, as many as six in a line, but that they generally worked in pairs. He says the last oxen used in Roxburghshire worked on a farm called Redden, near Carham.

A parishioner tells me that from her grandmother she used to hear about oxen ploughing, and that they used four oxen to a plough, in two pairs, one pair behind the other, the eight forming a yoke. Andrew Mattison, of Coldstream, tells me that in his young days, sixty years ago, he saw oxen ploughing on a farm three miles from Earlston. It was after the general disuse of cattle for the purpose, but the farmer had some rough moorland to bring into cultivation, and he obtained two pair (half a yoke) of very large strong oxen for the work. It was a hard frost and no horses could have done it, but the oxen made nothing of it, going uphill as if they had nothing behind them. One pair of oxen worked five hours, then the other pair took their turn for the same time. Mattison's statement is interesting as that of an eye-witness of the use of oxen at the time of which he speaks. He also shows that a yoke of oxen in his day was known to consist of eight animals, as it had from the most ancient times. And although he speaks of the strength of oxen as greater than that of horses, he shows that their power of endurance was much sooner exhausted, as they could only work in relays for a limited number of hours.

This latter fact accounts for the number of oxen included in what was termed a yoke, which always consisted of eight, and in old Reports of agriculture one of the arguments in favour of the use of horses for ploughing was, that it was much less costly to keep fewer animals that could do the same amount of work, and that while oxen, four or three working in one plough, required an extra hand to act as goadsman, a pair of animals could be guided by cords from the hands of the ploughman. The question of cost was chiefly between the higher price of horses compared with oxen, and also between the profit derived from grazing oxen and their use in labour. It was a complicated question, and so we find that in some cases in Northumberland the use of oxen was retained for purposes of carting after the general use of horses had begun (2).

Farming in Northumberland has had a high character, and modern methods have been adopted readily from their first introduction, and the use of oxen is now a somewhat dim tradition. Their use is generally a sign of a backward state of agriculture, and of the poverty of the farmer, as may be seen on the peasant farms in Germany, in the valleys and on the tablelands bordering the Rhine.

There are counties in England, however, where for special reasons their use is still retained (3). There are those who remember when the ox team was the rule in Sussex and horses the exception. In the year 1905 there were still some teams at work on the farms in the neighbourhood of Lewes.

I am told by a parishioner that she had a letter fourteen years ago from a friend who wrote, "I can look into Gloucestershire from my window and see the oxen ploughing in the fields."

I have heard Hertfordshire and Devonshire mentioned as still

58

continuing the use of working oxen, and they were used in Wiltshire six or seven years ago. Within living memory oxen were used for ploughing at Heanton Court Farm, North Devon.

I am told by a friend, now over eighty, that as a boy he heard from an old ploughman that either the ploughman or the goadsman "hummed a tune, a kind of sing-song, all day long, which soothed the oxen and made them docile, they seemed to work to it." We have in this a lingering tradition of a still earlier time alluded to by James Thomson, the poet, when calling up the memory of scenes in his youthful days at Southdean Manse, near Jedburgh.

SPRING, 1728.

"Joyous, th' impatient husbandman perceived
Relenting Nature, and his lusty steers
Drives from their stalls, to where the well used plough
Lies in the furrow; loosen'd from the frost.
There, unrefusing, to the harness'd yoke
They lend their shoulder, and begin their toil,
Cheer'd by the simple song and soaring lark.
Meanwhile, incumbent o'er the shining share
The master leans, removes the obstructing clay,
Winds the whole work, and sidelong lays the glebe."

(1) A writer in the *Home and Farm*, in a recent number of that paper, says apparently they can only be accounted for as an outcome of what one may call "the wisdom of the ancients. . . . . Certainly men who were born in the end of the century before last have told me that even their fathers and grandfathers could not give reasons for the practice. I know a field . . . . called 'Creamy Rigs ' where they are certainly three feet high from furrow to crown and it is a fact that I have demonstrated that a big bullock may lie four ridges from you and you can't see him, when standing in the furrow with his head down."

(2) General View of The Agriculture of Northumberland, by J Bailey and G. Culley, 1797.

CHAPTER IX.

Shepherding.

Even the most careless observer passing along the main road, which runs through our valley, must perceive that at the present day, it is a pastoral, more than an agricultural country.

Barley and oats still cover many fields with tender green in early spring, but the best, the most cherished, and the most profitable crop, is the "crop of lambs" that you see rejoicing with their mothers in the spacious meadows of sweet young grass. For many a year I had seen the same fields and uplands peopled with their flocks, but never had the lambs seemed so greatly to outnumber the ewes: then came from shepherds and farmers the admission that it was a record crop. On one farm there are sixty more lambs than in the previous year. A shepherd in our village has a ewe with five lambs doing well. In 1906 she had four and in 1905 five; fourteen lambs in three years. This surely is very remarkable. It seems that as time goes on, and the feeding and care of sheep are better understood, they become more prolific. Single lambs are becoming quite the exception in our Northumberland farms.

It is early in May, and the freshly washed "hogs," as the one year old sheep are called, shine white in the sun in contrast to the young grass over which the flock is scattered.

It is a little too cold to wash the ewes, but their lambs are getting strong and big, and so their time will soon come to take their jump into the stream, their short swim to the bank, and then their quick run to join their bleating companions in the pen. This "jumping " process, which is repeated twice, and sometimes three times, is the modern method, and is considered quite as effectual as the old plan of hand washing, in which the shepherd stood waist high in the water, and with great labour plunged the sheep under water, and swayed it to and fro, before releasing it for its final swim out and its clamber up the bank.

In a fortnight the harvest of shining fleeces you see in the field will be gathered in. With us it is the corn that is shorn. Sheep are not shorn but "clipped," but still it is the shears that clips them, and the harvest of wool is called "the clip". The shears will not cut the wool until about two weeks after washing, for the water has washed out the "eck," or natural oil, that it contained. When the "eck " returns the clipping can begin. And in this, hand labour still holds its own.

A SMALL FAMILY OF FOUR ON FLODDON FARM, 1907.

And here as in hand sowing, we have ambidextrousness. Half the fleece is clipped with the left hand, and half with the right at least on our lowland farms, where the finest breeds of sheep are kept; but "out bye," on the hill farms of the Cheviot slopes, only the right hand is used. The Cheviot sheep is more difficult to clip, the wool is matted and tough; it is not clipped close, but a little thickness is left as a protection against the colder climate of the hills.

Another curious difference is, that while the lowland sheep are clipped in the direction of the ribs upwards, the hill sheep are clipped lengthways down the back and across the ribs. You may easily see this by the furrows left by the shears after clipping, which leave a regular series of rings around the body, in the case of our well bred sheep.

In the hills the large flocks are clipped by the friendly cooperation of neighbours, who meet to do the work, receiving only hospitality in return ; this is the constant custom.

Farming is often spoken of lightly, as if it were merely a pleasant occupation upon which anyone feeling a taste for it may enter. When, however, it is properly considered, and its various branches, on farms, where there is both stock and crop, the wonder is that even wise and clever management can carry it on with such success as we often see.

If you did not know that a good deal of barley and corn were still grown, and that one very large branch of our farming was the feeding of cattle you might suppose, especially at this season of the year, that the breeding and feeding of sheep was the one occupation of our farmers. It is not so, but still, it is true that the pastoral branch is, with us, certainly, the most in evidence, and not the least profitable. The flock occupies as large a space in the farmer's thoughts as his fields. To supply the flock with food, in spite of all the rich meadows of summer, there must be continuous work throughout the year. The coming of May sees the last of the turnips eaten, in sight of the next field in which all hands are engaged in sowing the seed for another season. What splendid drills those are, how straight they run, how well they are ridged up. A stranger would almost think they were prepared for some military purpose, so precise and thorough is the work all over the many acred field. Each ridge, too, is well manured below, and over and along each, the women workers walk, with quick step and active sweep of the hand, sowing a dust of guano, or some other substance to cause a rapid growth of the young plant when it comes up. There is no carelessness in cultivating this crop, and no expense spared to attain success. And yet there is no crop that gives the farmer such anxiety. Turnips are not indigenous to Northumberland, nor are they suited to its dry cold springs, but Northumberland, owing to the enterprise of its farmers, has splendid flocks, and so, at any cost, it must have good store of turnips to feed them during its long winters.

The care and feeding of these fine flocks is the occupation most in evidence on our farms. In winter the feeding of cattle, in spacious byres, goes on daily with great labour, but this is not seen by the outsider. Sheep, however, are always in the open and the process of feeding them during the long winter months, is a constant and familiar sight. If the little turnips come up after the first sowing, and escape the drought and frost, and their insect enemies, "singling" soon begins. The whole force of women workers, as at the sowing, appear upon the scene, with the steward at their head. With a deft movement of the hoe backwards and forwards, they clear away the superfluous plants, leaving the little seedlings at equal distances apart, limp and forlorn, drooping over the ridge, with tender stem exposed, but soon to recover themselves, the roots being well established in the prepared soil.

And then, with the interval of the hay, corn, and potato harvests, and the cutting of thistles in the fields, November comes, and women again appear on the scene to pull the turnips, to cut away the green tops with a chopper before they are stored, and, month after month, to feed the sheep, until May returns again.

With us, the shepherd herds and breeds the sheep, but it is the shepherdess who does the hard work of winter feeding. And this work must go on in all weathers. Be the frost keen, or the west wind boisterous, or the north wind cruel, there in the open field is the woman laboriously turning the crank handle of the turnip cutter, lifting the heavy box of food, and supplying her eager flock. If anything is more characteristic than another of our Border farms, it is this picture of the woman and the turnip cutter. Our flocks of the present day owe, for their quality and value, as much to the shepherdess who feeds them, as to the shepherd who herds, and pastures, doctors, and buys and sells them. So rapidly does today become yesterday in the advance of agricultural machinery that women will soon have relief from this heavy labour of turning the crank handle of the turnip cutter and lifting the boxes of food. A machine has lately come into use on many farms that travels about the field cutting the turnips it contains by the force of the revolution of its wheels and at the same time conveying the cut food to the sheep troughs.

But it is the shepherd who has the responsibility, and no little arduous labour, and many a night of watching by the fold, when the lambs come, in the ice-cold weather of earliest spring. The fold of straw and hurdles is a good "beild" (shelter) against snow showers and piercing winds, and the shepherd generally has his wooden hut. He is hardy, and used to his laborious life; but more than this, he is interested in his work, and takes a pride in it. The fact is, he is a prospective farmer himself. His wages are excellent, and the knowledge and experience he acquires in his calling are of great commercial value. Probably he has "stock wages," that is, the greater part of his wages paid in "kind." In that case, he will be allowed to keep and feed, with his master's grass and winter fodder, about 18 ewes of his own, the number of the shepherd's sheep depending on the quality of the pasture of the farm. He is paid besides about £16 a year in money instead of the old allowance of meal and beans, and has the keep of a cow, and 1,800 yards of potatoes, with a free house, like the hinds. When the value of sheep is high, and the price of wool is good, stock wages are much preferred by shepherds, and this method of payment is again becoming very general, as it did when many years ago the breeding and feeding of sheep began to be so much improved. Some farmers object to the system, and prefer to give money wages, as they find winter feeding becomes more costly. They may also possibly imagine that the shepherd's flock may receive more care than their own. It is most likely, however, that as all the sheep are fed and pastured together, the shepherd would be more anxious to do his duty by the whole, because his own formed a part, of the flock.

The Cheviot shepherds are allowed to keep a much larger number of sheep of their own; they have no money wages, but, on the other hand, they are allowed to keep large flocks of geese and much other poultry, a privilege which is denied to our farm servants, and to most of our villagers.

Shepherding with stock wages is thus a very successful example of the working of the co-operative principle, in a friendly form with free contract, and seems to act fairly to both employer and employed. But because it answers with this one branch of farming, it does not follow that it would succeed with the much more complicated, and more costly work of arable farming.

The interest of the profit sharing shepherd in his work raises him quite above the hireling, and makes him the trusted fellow worker with the farmer.

In sermons we often hear that the toils and dangers of an Eastern shepherd are greater than those experienced at home. But anyone really acquainted with the work of the shepherd, either of our large and valuable lowland flocks, or his still more exposed life on the Cheviot slopes, will think differently. If there are not wild beasts, there are sheep-worrying dogs that may do a hundred pounds' worth of damage in a night.

There is the "big" water to watch in the spring rains, or it will carry part of the flock through Till and Tweed to the North Sea. And there is the sudden blizzard, leaving deep snow drifts, which are a peril to sheep and shepherd alike.

I have heard of a collie who was a trained sheep stealer. His master would take him to a spot a long distance from some flock, would make some signal with his arm, and the dog would take a wide circuit and single one sheep out and bring it to his master. After the man died the dog gave up the practice, which shows that he acted only at the instigation of his dishonest master. The cleverness of these dogs is wonderful, and the stories the shepherds relate about them would fill a volume. But of course such stories are very like one another. They tell of dogs that know their own flock so well that they will separate it from any other in the crowded mart; of dogs that have saved sheep from drowning in the rapid current of the water; of dogs that will go and pull a sheep over when struggling on its back.

The collie knows the individual sheep of the flock perhaps better than the shepherd, but the shepherd of to-day has the same wonderful power of knowing his own sheep from others as the shepherd of Holy Writ, and that not by any mark that they may bear, but by their individuality. To the outsider, one looks just like another, but to the shepherd, who is constantly with them, they differ as much as human beings, especially in the shape of the head and the outline and expression of the face.

One still hears traditions of the old sheep-stealing days: they are mere fragments, but they have come down by word of mouth. At one farm two of the hinds were out in the field eating their dinner, which generally would he of a very simple description, certainly without "butchers meat," but, one of them, who was very poor, was well supplied with mutton, much to the surprise of his companion, who remarked upon it. The guilty one replied, "Ah, if this mutton could speak it could tell a queer tale."

In the old droving days before the railway came, immense herds of cattle and sheep were driven southward through the unenclosed country. One old inn in our parish still has a room containing the beds on which the drovers used to sleep. One of these men was in a cottage receiving the hospitality of the inmates. He said that he was once in charge of a big drove of sheep, and being tired he lay down to rest near a hedge. He saw some men come towards the flock, but was himself unobserved. One of them began to take away, or, as we say here, to "lift" a sheep. The drover suddenly rose up and cried out, "Where's the money? you've no' paid the money for the ewe, man." The remark was too civil for the occasion, but it had the desired effect, and the thieves, taken by surprise, quickly decamped. The following is a copy of an old printed notice found a short time ago in the drawer of an old bookcase bought at a sale. It shows that down to the year 1828 sheep stealing was so prevalent in this region, and constables were so few, that even in our little village there existed an association for the prosecution of felons, which was able to offer large rewards for that object:-

FIFTEEN POUNDS REWARD.
SHEEP STOLEN.
WHEREAS on Tuesday night last, or early on Wednesday morning, a ewe sheep, the property of Mr. Carr, was slaughtered in a field adjoining Flodden Hill Plantation; the entrails and skin were found deposited amongst some whins in the Plantation,- Notice is hereby given, that a reward of Ten Pounds is offered by the Ford Association (for the Prosecution of Felons); and a further sum of Five Pounds will be given by the said Mr. Carr to any Person or Persons who can give such information as will lead to the Conviction of the Offender or Offenders.
C. RICHARDSON,
Printer,
Berwick.
Ford, *August 22nd,* 1828.

It sometimes happens that a lamb of one family has to be placed under the care of a mother not its own. Among the different ways of bringing about this adoption, and reconciling the ewe to her new charge, the following plan is sometimes successful. The ewe and lamb are for some days penned together. They are then liberated, and a collie is set on to give them a good chase about the field. This arouses the protective instinct, and the ewe does battle with the dog to shield the lamb. After this she takes it as her own. It is chiefly in difficult cases that this plan is pursued.

Twice a year "Cheviot's mountain lone" is enlivened with a great gathering of the hill shepherds, and the bleating of many sheep. One meeting takes place on the very top of Cheviot on the 10th of July, the other on the 10th of November, lower down near the foot of the mountain. There are generally about 30 to 40 shepherds present, and sometimes 400 sheep to be exchanged. The day begins with sports, for our hill shepherd is a great lover of sport. The real purpose, however, of these meetings is to restore lost sheep to their proper owners. Many a stray sheep gets far away from its proper feeding ground to another where it does not belong, these are looked after by each shepherd until the half-yearly exchange takes place. Some of the poor things when brought in look very forlorn, and sometimes have a two or a three year's growth of wool on them. After the shepherds have claimed their own, the flock is separated, and moves off in three general divisions, in the direction of the valleys of the Breamish, the College, and the Coquet, to be again and again sub-divided, as each small detachment nears its own feeding ground.

Meetings of this sort are no doubt common to all wide moorland tracts of country, and they are held in Cumberland, but there, and in Westmorland, the sheep of each owner wander freely over a wide district and for the most part return of themselves to their homeland, at the same season each year

67

CHAPTER X.

Vanished and Vanishing Industries.

While sitting the other day in one of the picturesque thatched cottages of our village, I was surprised to hear that it had been once a milliner's shop. It has now a very small window, but then it had a wide window in which Margaret Gibson used to display straw bonnets and hats to suit all tastes. They were made of rye straw, plaited in a neighbouring village. Some were of coarse texture, for bonnets to wear in field work, Some were more finely wrought, for Sundays and holidays. Lent was a busy time for Margaret, because every girl in the village and neighbouring farm places had a new rig-out for Easter, and each watched impatiently for the appearance of her new bonnet in the window. They would eagerly enquire of one another "Is my bonnet up yet?" Very natural was this excitement as the new headgear was to last with occasional alterations and new trimmings until Easter came round again. But the bonnet was a durable thing in those days, and not less becoming because it was a useful covering for the head, both in summer and winter. Even the young field workers have far higher wages now, but as their mothers sometimes remind them, their money is spent in trivial finery rather than in serviceable garments.

The spinning wheel has, of course, long ago departed. It does not remain even as a curiosity. The "little wheel" on which the flax, here always called lint, was spun, was the first to go, but there are those amongst us who still remember its use. The wives of the hinds were obliged to spin, in the farmhouse, a certain weight of "lint" every year for the farmer's wife, and to supply this, there was a plot of lint grown at each of the farms. There is a farm in our valley on the flat land near the river called the "Lint Haugh," a permanent record of flax growing.

As the flax had to be steeped in running water and "swingled" or thrashed to prepare it for the "little wheel," so the wool for home use had to be carded before it could be spun on the "long wheel." The carding or combing was often done at home with metal combs, but there still remains by the river side a building which was the carding mill of the district, worked by water power. To this the raw wool was brought. Often it was in small quantities, gleaned in the fields chiefly by the children of the family, with the farmers' full permission; gathered from the thorn hedges and from the stubble and grass all over the fields. There was then a literal "wool gathering," but the term now has only its very expressive metaphorical sense. In the evening by the cottage fire the children would again be busy, teasing out the wool they had gathered, and putting it into bags hung on either side the hearth, to be ready for the mill when filled. The wool left the carding mill cleansed and teased into a continuous and beautiful coil, ready to be put on the distaff and drawn out by the "long wheel" into worsted thread.

In connection with the carding mill there was a field which is still called the "bleach" field where wool was bleached, and also cotton cloth, then called calico. Another large business carried on at the same river-side hamlet was the scouring of blankets. Great quantities of these were supplied by the farmers to the Irish labourers, who were employed in great numbers for many weeks in summer. These blankets were called "sheards." They were not washed at home, but sent after harvest to the mill to be scoured. This was called the "walk mill," as the blankets were trodden with the feet, as women now often wash clothes in Scotland. The dyeing of yarn and cloth was also carried on here.

But there were two other flourishing industries at this point on our river, which gave a great number of hands employment. On one side the stream was harnessed to a forge, and on the other side to a flour mill. The forge, built by the owner of the estate, was at first a simple blacksmith's shop. In 1788 it was taken by an enterprising tenant. He found that besides other things, there was a demand for spades and shovels. A few of these were at first made entirely by hand and sold at St Ninian's Fair, the great annual meeting-place of the farmers of the district. The demand for these tools soon became greater, and a heavy upright hammer worked by a water wheel was obtained. This was used to forge the tools in the rough. The finishing process was carried on in a large workshop having several forges.

At this forge were made axes, sledge-hammers, hedge-cutting bills, and all sorts of farm and garden implements. Someone was not pleased with a plough he had purchased, and complained of it as defective, and told the proprietor that he could not make a plough. "I can make a plough," replied the master, "but I cannot make a man to go with her," There were several smiths and apprentices employed, and a fine set of men they were. In the early days of this business a bar of iron was given to a man and he was able to complete the spade from first to last, having learnt during his five years apprenticeship every process of its manufacture. It is true the division of labour soon began in a modified form, and there were four processes, each one allotted to a different set of men but all was hand work except that of the forge hammer. In the making of a spade in the works of the same firm now transferred to a neighbouring town, there are no less than sixteen separate processes, all done by machinery, and not a man in the place is able to make and finish a spade. This is perhaps as good an illustration as one could get of the disastrous effect of machinery upon the worker, who himself becomes a mere machine. Intelligence and skill are no longer required or exerted. All is monotony and drudgery. The dignity of labour and honest pride in good work can no longer exist. It may seem vain to say this, but whatever be the advantages of machinery, all must own that it has its dark side in the present, and holds out no cheerful prospect in the future.

The contrast of past and present is very striking as you look upon this Till-side hamlet. Seventy years ago it was a busy hive of industry with seven water-wheels, supplied with power that would have driven seven more, and with over thirty houses inhabited by smiths, millers and carters. It is now desolate, its forges unused, its habitable houses reduced to five, its massive flour mill grinding only grist for cattle. The big hammer, which used to work day and night, no longer gives life to the valley by its measured thud heard for many a mile along the grinding stream. To those who were accustomed to its sound softened by distance, its silence still seems like the stopping of the tick of the eight day clock to the cottager, or the sudden ceasing of the engines on an ocean boat; a silence that may be felt, possibly ominous of something wrong.

On the opposite side of the river stands the mill which in the days of corn wages did a great trade. To it the "batcher," the mill carter, brought all the portions of corn from the hinds' houses, and when ground, he took them back again minus the miller's "Mouter," so much from every bushel. In the case of oats, however, when ground into oat meal, a message was sent to each house from which it had come, telling its owner to come or send on a certain day to see the meal weighed. The hinds' wives generally came to claim their portion. Part of it they sold to the miller for money, or exchanged for other provisions; the rest was sent home. The women, no doubt, enjoyed their little outing, for, on these days, they had a tea party at the foreman miller's house, his wife being allowed one or two young pigs each year for her trouble.

The business of the forge and the mill involved a great deal of carting. Iron had to be brought from a distance, and coal from the local collieries. Carting was of itself a flourishing industry even thirty years ago. Motoring would be difficult if our deserted roads had the same cart traffic on them now. Several of my parishioners remember that there were eighty cart horses kept in one of our villages, which now boasts of only two. But those were the days when our vast stores of lime were utilized for the fields, and hundreds of carts came to the kilns and took it away to all the farms on the Border. The empty cart would go at a quick pace to get a good position at the kiln the night before, and return laden in the early hours of the morning. Many a time was one's sleep broken by their continuous rumbling. In those days it was quite easy for a mother to get from passing carts a "lime shell" (or lump of unslaked lime) to make lime water to mix with her baby's milk, but now it must be bought at the chemist's eight miles distant and brought by the postman.

Our local collieries were thought to be of some use in those days, and worth the working. The Lord of the manor used to say that his coal pit was the best farm on the estate. Indeed, it must have been, for the amount of coal cartage was enormous, and it was taken far into Scotland by our carters.

The lime quarries still exist, and the fields need lime more than ever they did. The coal exists too, and every ton of it would he eagerly bought: the best seams have never been worked. We cannot blame the railways for the disuse of lime, or for the famine of coal that we sometimes have to face in our cold and snowy winters. How the farmers do without lime which twenty-five years ago was considered essential to the land, it is hard to know, but never a load of it now comes from kiln or railway station, unless it be to make mortar.

With the disappearance of carts, except those kept by the farmers, and one or two in each village, the trade of our wheelwrights came

71

to a standstill, and there were two wheelwrights shops in one of our villages. You do still see the old thatched building where this trade once flourished, and at long intervals a cart wheel fresh with vermilion paint will be leaning against the wall. I have seen a new made wheelbarrow standing outside the place as if it would say, "Hard wood still exists, and you can have a good hand-made barrow if you specially order it." Enter the door of the shop and chat with the now ageing representative of the old firm. He will tell you in a few sentences enough to give food for reflection during your three mile walk home and after. He and his father and brothers were all hard-working carpenters and wheelwrights. They used to make all the cottage furniture: the box-bed, the dresser, and the meal chest, when a young couple set up house. It was the custom for the carpenter to add to these plenishings a present for the bride, of a "buffette stool" and a rolling pin. The "buffette stool" is of solid construction, with two legs consisting of sloping boards, kept in position by being fastened to two side pieces connected with the top. The top of the stool has a hole in the centre so that it can be lifted by the finger. This hole is sometimes round but generally heart shaped. The sides are scalloped with rather nice curves. In a cottage you will always see this stool, and also a wee stool with four sloping legs, called a "cracket" or "cracky stool," for the very small children.

Carts and cart-wheels are now made almost wholly by machinery. Those "felloes" that you see there, are of elm, a very tough wood, generally used for the rim of the wheel. They were cut out by machinery at Kelso: but our friend, when he does make a wheel, will put them together. The nave and spokes will be made of American oak. English oak is not much used now for this purpose. It is far better and more durable, but harder to work and more costly. "This," says our friend, "is a wheel spoke of English oak, cut from a tree on the estate thirty years ago. You see, as I run the plane over it, what a fine grain and colour it has. Such spokes were not cut out of planks from the tree, but out of wedge shaped sections, as you would cut into a round pie. There was a good deal of waste with this method, but the wood was better, and you got the finest grain that way, if you desired it for any special purpose. Hand work," he continued, "is far and away better than machine work: when a man handles a piece of wood he finds out any defect

A FIELD WORKER

Ploughing.

The Cheviot Hills.

By permission of Mr. John Worsnop.]

A Group of Field Workers.

[Photographer, Rothbury.

Twisted or Lang Sync Rigs.

A Northumberland Harvest Scene.

Hand Sowing.

Coldstream Bridge Inn (Marriage House).

in it, and rejects it ; a machine does not discover the defect, but works up good and bad material alike."

In the same village with our wheelwright there were no less than five saw-pits, of which no traces now exist. Three of the old sawyers I well remember. They were very tall, spare men, who lived to a good age; but their occupation was most laborious, and one cannot help feeling that the invention of the circular saw was a great boon.

With the disappearance of carters there was no longer sufficient trade in harness, and so when our one saddler died, no one continued the business. He used not only to work at home but went to farmsteads to repair harness. It was really good to see an honest piece of solid leather hanging up in his room. There was good leather also to be seen in those days in the cottages of our village cobblers. I am told that in 1845 there were in the village of Etal no less than five shoemakers doing a thriving trade, and four tailors. Now in 1907 there are no shoemakers and no cobblers in either of the three villages in our parish. What is the consequence? Whereas formerly our workers were able to have solid handmade boots and clogs, made under their own supervision, and suited to their work in field or garden, they are now obliged to buy whatever in the way of footwear is sent to them from towns, and they are not able to get the least bit of cobbling done without the expense of postage.

We still have the village tailor. There is now work for one or two tailors in a parish which used to keep six or seven busily engaged. In those days this business was carried on chiefly at the houses of the customers, who were for the most part hinds at the farm cottages. The tailor was paid two shillings a day and his food, and if he took an apprentice with him, which he generally did, the apprentice received one shilling. The employer supplied the cloth for the family suits. It was generally bought from travelling packmen, who carried a yard measure, as a walking stick, and as the ostensible emblem of their trade; but they were often as much smugglers of whisky as they were cloth merchants. A good deal of the cloth used came from wool grown on the farms, and woven either in the village, or at mills not far off. The coming of the tailor was hailed with delight by the younger members of the hind's family, for he generally remained three days, and in addition to the prospect of new clothes, there was the more immediate satisfaction

73

of much better fare than usual on the family board, although the expression still extant, "tailor's hash," shows that its quality deteriorated towards the end of the time. It used to be the boast of some of these tradesmen that on reaching a house where they were to work, they only needed to cast a look around at the family to enable them to take the correct measure of the men and boys. A tailor once came to our village from London, where he had learned his trade, and carried himself rather haughtily towards his country brethren of the craft. To one of them he once said, and probably with perfect truth, "I can make a good-fitting suit for any man if I only see him in the road." But our country friend was ready with the answer, "Ay, but just tell me where a man lives, and I could do the same."

TAILOR'S EMBLEMS ON TOMBSTONE.

74

The old practice of making the clothes of the family at the house of the customer has almost died out. It went by the name of "whipping the cat." A man who now works at the trade at home will say, "I whipped the cat " for so many years. The origin of this expression is obscure, and the people who use it cannot throw any light upon it.

Horse-shoe Door of Blacksmith's Forge.

75

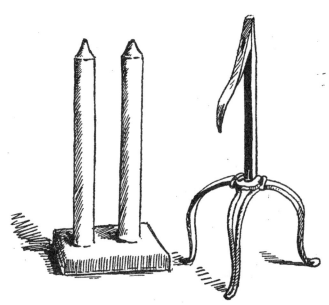

CANDLE MOULD AND RUSHLIGHT HOLDER.

With all our present advantages in the matter of lighting our houses, streets, railway carriages and ocean steamers, it is somewhat difficult to realize that there are still many people living who well remember the days when candle making was a domestic industry, and each household made its yearly supply of rushlights, dips and mould candles. It could hardly have been a pleasant operation, for the material used was the accumulated fat of sheep that had died on the farm during the year and had been boiled down. The simplest manner of making dip candles was this. Two long handled hay forks were laid side by side resting on chairs or some other supports. Across these were placed a number of sticks from which hung the cotton wicks. When the cauldron of boiling fat was ready, each member of the family would seize one of these rods, dip

76

the line of suspended wicks into the fat and replace it. This was done very quickly as the fat soon cooled in the cauldron, and it took many dips to make a substantial candle. When several hands were at work, and such rapid action was required, it was natural that there should be some excitement and merriment among the young people of the household. It is no doubt this bit of fun over the candle making, which the young enjoyed, that has made the memory of it in the old so distinct.

Following the age of dips, came mould candles, which was also a cottage industry. The moulds were made of tin, sometimes for a single candle, sometimes for two, four, six or eight in a cluster. Before the boiling fat was poured in they were imbedded in sand, to support them in an upright position, the ends being uppermost, and terminating in a small tray which received the fat and conveyed it into the tubes. When cool the candles were easily drawn out, as the moulds were tapered from the bottom upwards. In the days of dips when coin was scarce, but each house was provided with its yearly supply of candles, which hung in bundles from the rafters, as the bacon still hangs, the men would often carry a bundle of dips with them to the public house, with which to pay their score or to settle a wager.

Another home-made article was soap, made of sheep's fat, soda and lime. I hear that at one farm near us soap was made regularly until four years ago, and probably is made there now.

Yeast is still made in a few of our cottages by thrifty people who supply their own wants, and sell it to a neighbour or two. It is made of hops, sugar, flour, and a little old yeast to leaven it. Those who make and use it say that bread made with it does not get nearly so dry as that made with so-called German yeast. The latter, however, has the advantage that it causes the bread to rise more quickly. With home-made yeast the bread needs to be set to rise over night. The German yeast sold at our village shop does not come from Germany, but is made in Edinburgh.

No doubt our railways, indispensable as they are in many ways, must bear no small part of the blame of destroying our country industries. They centralize, instead of localizing, trade. One is inclined to think that it is better to have no railways, or else to have a great many more of them. No railways meant local industry, and self-supporting communities. Insufficient railway communication means the desolation and poverty of one district, to the advantage of another. At one point on our section of the London and Edinburgh road, there may be seen an extensive range of red tiled buildings and a tall chimney. No smoke has come from the chimney for some years. It is many years since smoke came from it in any volume. The place is called the tile shades, because, besides bricks, and the dear old roofing pantiles, a very large quantity of drain pipes were made there. In those days much money was spent in draining the land. Perhaps the urgent need of draining the land again may one day revive the industry, use up some of the abundant clay that surrounds the buildings, and cause the chimney to smoke again. But now all is silent and deserted; outside, only stacks of unsold bricks, and inside the drying sheds only the ghosts of the freshly made tiles, and bricks and flower pots, which during the latter days of the industry one used to see. No longer are any of these useful things made, nor burned in the kiln, nor glazed with the salt that was used for his purpose. No longer is there any workman there, as there used to be among the many hands employed, who can be tempted to mould the clay into milk pans, pitchers, or even higher flights of the potter's art. The kindly old man is dead who told me of the busy days of the tile shades, the days before the railways. He worked there himself; eighty men were employed, forty by night and forty by day. How the fire must have glowed in the furnaces then, and among the piled up bricks, how constantly must the smoke of the chimney have seen across the valley, and what a great traffic of carts there must have been along the road.

Chapter XI

Pastimes

It is often asserted that the dullness of rural life is one of the chief reasons for the migration of young people from the country to the town. But have those who say this considered whether the young men and women who leave their country homes really feel the dullness of their lives, or that they are to any extent attracted by the glamour of the city, as they hear of it from their friends or read of it in the newspapers. The country may seem dull to those who view the matter from their own standpoint, and not from that of the workers who form the bulk of the population, and constitute a far larger society than that of all the other classes put together. Even in such a district as ours with its greatly diminished population, scattered over a considerable area, there is a social life among the working class of wide extent, and the greatest interest to themselves. The Squire and the Parson may at times feel the want of society in a rural district, but not the farm workers or the villagers. It is true they do not very often meet but their acquaintance is large. The hind and his wife know the history of every other working family within several parishes. Their social life is fostered by the many interests they have in common. They meet at fairs, marts, sales, and local agricultural shows. In all these functions it is as much the meeting of friends and acquaintances as the business they may transact that is their object. The hiring days are of great importance to them, as then the fate of their families is settled for the coming year, but even these days are a sort of "gathering of the clans," and are of great social value to them, satisfying their gregarious instinct, which is remarkably strong. They love a crowd. A crowd is their idea of success, whether the object be a bazaar, a missionary meeting, or a service in church or chapel. If they go away saying, "What a people there was there!" you may know that your audience is satisfied.

Among those things which keep up the social unity of our people is their fondness for the dance, which is the most sociable of all amusements. In our case it is a striking instance of extremes meeting. You would never expect to find, in so reserved a race, slow of speech, deliberate of movement, a passionate love of dancing. But so it is. And they never tire of it. It is not a craze or fashion which lasts a winter or two and then fades away, until the interest in it is in time again revived. To meet together in the dance is with the Border people a strong hereditary taste. It is as much a passion as the instinct for fighting in warlike people. And it is doubtless quite as primitive. You seem to see, indeed, in the intricate figures of the reels and contra dances in which they delight, and the inspiriting shout and stampede which accompanies some of them, an evident reminiscence of the ancient war dance. And one might easily believe that some of the circular dances, such as the Pin Reel, were remnants of the ritual of the worship of the Sun. Here, at any rate, you have an ancient custom in full force at the present day, a thing in which our working people are intensely interested, and of which, although a sober and serious race, they thoroughly approve. It is not easy as a rule to get people to amuse themselves, but here is an innocent amusement, always successful, and only needing proper management and supervision to render it a most elevating social influence. It is a marvellous thing, this spirit and enthusiasm with which our border people give themselves up to dancing. The tidings of a coming dance stir them up as nothing else will. Very few will decline your invitation, and although you will be careful to choose a moonlight night for your ball, you need not think that either darkness, distance, or bad weather will prevent the arrival of your guests. And when all have come, and the Master of Ceremonies announces the first dance, what a transformation scene it all is compared with the work-a-day world which the young people have for a few bright hours left behind them. There is nobility in all labour, but a stranger to our country looking at our guests taking their partners at the sound of the first strains of the "Triumph" country dance, would never suppose that these well dressed and well mannered young people represent the real workers of our countryside. How different those tastefully made light dresses, to the usual costume of the field worker. How immense the contrast must be to those girls, the brightness, warmth and movement of the ballroom, with the dull and cold routine of cutting turnips on the bleak hillside, or feeding cattle in the byres. Our friends from the South, who sometimes attend our balls, are surprised by their heartiness, and greatly interested in them. They naturally enquire how the people obtain and keep up the knowledge

80

of the many complicated dances which our programmes contain. Probably the farm kirn or harvest-home party, a very ancient custom still observed, has kept alive this knowledge.

There has long been a practice at the farms for the young people of the farmsteads to have an occasional dance in the open air of an evening, in any open ground there may be adjoining the cottages. Such dancing in isolated farm places is not to be commended, as it takes place generally on winter nights by candle light, and without any supervision by the elder folks; but the practice proves how strong the passion for this amusement is, and that it forms a natural antidote to the laborious lives of the people. This practice has, no doubt, helped to keep up the knowledge of dances which, although not always so light and graceful as those of southern countries, are yet wonderfully complicated in their figures and steps, and, to a looker-on, picturesque to a degree.

There are still many who remember the visits to our villages of the travelling dancing master. These were men of the working class, and often of an idle jovial disposition, fond of dancing, and good fiddlers. The travelling dancing master would stay in the village for two or three months in the winter, and give his lessons in a hired room, or a loft lent for the purpose. The members of the class and a few friends paid him a small sum. From time to time he gave a more public dance, which he called "a small occasion," and at the close of the season "a grand ball" for his own benefit. This practice was long in vogue, and no doubt it did much to preserve the knowledge of the old Border and Scotch dances. It ceased in the English Border about thirty years ago, but is still maintained in some parts of Scotland. Since the establishment of Reading Rooms, which now exist even in our smallest villages, their committees often organize public dances. Rut these cannot be so beneficial as private balls given by the Parson or Lord of the manor, under their own management and supervision.

The music for our balls is supplied by one of five fiddlers of the district, who is seated on a chair raised aloft upon a table, which forms the minstrels' gallery for the time being. He always has with him an assistant, who takes his place when he needs rest or refreshment. It cannot be said that our borderers are a musical people, and yet it would be difficult to find in any part of England, in the same area, so many who play the violin, as far at least as

81

dance music is concerned. They do not profess to be more than fiddlers, and many of them keep good time and tune, and find the winter a profitable season. It seems a pity that even this talent should not be further cultivated, and our church and chapel music varied by the addition of stringed instruments, as in the days before organs dominated the choir.

PROGRAMME OF DANCES IN FORD VILLAGE, 1905-1907.

Triumph.... Contra Dance.
Plain Schottische.
Polka.
Waltz.
Reel O Tulloch or Hooligan.
Barn Dance.
Quadrille.
Highland Schottische.
My love she's but a lassie yet.
Ribbon Dance . (1)
Heel and Toe Polka.
Circassian Circle.
Scotch Reel, *The Reel* Strathspey and Reel danced to the tunes of "Harvest Home" and "Harvest lang a' coming."

Lancers.
Patronella,' Contra Dance, to "Highland Laddie" tune.
Dutch Polka.' (1)
Nancy Till.' (1)
Pin Reel, danced by nine persons, one forming the pin in the centre of tile circle.
Leap Year Polka.
Spanish Waltz. (1)
Roxburgh Castle. (1)
Hornpipe and Highland Fling, in interludes.
God Save the King.
Auld Lang Syne.

PROGRAMME or DANCES IN FORD VILLAGE 85 YEARS Ago.

The Reel.
The Reel o' 'Tulloch.
Sixsome Reel.
Reel of Tullo'goram.
Ninesome Reel.

Strathspey.
Newcastle Honpipe.
Berwick Johnnie(Hornpipe).
Sailor's Hornpipe.

Little seems to be known of the history of the dances most in vogue on the English Border. The greater number are Scotch Reels, Strathspeys, and Country Dances. It is interesting to find that the Reel is the Danish as well as the Scottish National Dance (2). But there are some other dances here which have a marked individuality of their own, and this makes one curious to know their origin. There is what is called in our programmes the Spanish Waltz. Its name, as well as its steps and figures, show it to be foreign. It is not a waltz at all, but at one stage the dancers do join hands, and as they turn wave their arms gracefully up and down in quite an un-English fashion. There can be little doubt that this is the Saraband (3) which Sir George Grove says is probably Eastern. It is found in Europe at the beginning of the 16th century. It was a court dance in Spain. In England it was soon transformed into an ordinary country dance.

The Ribbon Dance is also very interesting and distinctive, and surely must have a history. The partners stand in opposite rows holding ribbons of various bright colours which cross the space between, and the dance consists chiefly in the partners successively passing under the ribbon that is held by the couple at the end. The Ribbon dance is very pleasant to watch, especially if seen at the end of the rows of dancers, where the effect is that of the interweaving of bright colours, bending forms, and happy faces. It is sometimes called the Handkerchief Dance, but without coloured ribbons it loses something of its brightness and originality.

The Reel O' Tulloch, otherwise called the Hooligan or Hoolakin (a Gaelic word) is a rather rough and noisy dance, but one always included in our programmes. It is a great favourite, and is danced with tremendous energy and spirit.

The Pin Reel is a circular dance, but also somewhat rough. Whatever be its origin or history it would seem to be characteristic of those ancient dances of imitation in which capture for marriage is represented. It is always danced once at least during the evening.

The Highland Schottische (4) was originally a martial dance, and women did not engage in it.

The Varsoviana (5) is probably of Polish origin. It was much danced at the Tuileries balls, and is said to have been a great favourite with the Empress Eugenie (6).

There is a dance called the Cushion Dance which often comes at the conclusion of kirns or harvest balls, and which deserves notice. The chief feature is the action of individual dancers. The man, or woman, as the case may be, dancing about, places a cushion at the feet of a chosen partner, kneels upon it. and as a suppliant receives a kiss. Meanwhile, the rest of the company dance in a ring singing :-

"The best bed, the feather bed
The best bed ov a';
The best bed i' wor hoose
Is clean pea straw" (7)

The person giving the kiss then takes up the cushion in turn and repeats the ceremony with another, all singing the refrain

"That dance of dances, the cushion dance."

This dance may to some appear homely and somewhat unsuited to the manners of the present day, but its history shows us, that like several other dances of the North, it was once in high favour with all classes (8). "In Queen Elizabeth's time it was performed at Court with great gravity and solemnity by all the company, lords and ladies, grooms and kitchen maids. It continued to be a favourite all through the century." It was then called Joan Sanderson, and the song was a dialogue between the person who is the suppliant and the musician. The dancer with the cushion sings (7) "This dance it will no further go," to which the musician answers: "I pray you, good sir, why say you so." "Because Joan Sanderson will not come to." "She must come to whether she will or no" returns the musician, and then the dancer lays the cushion before a woman; she kneels and he kisses her, singing, "Welcome, Joan Sanderson." Then she rises, takes up the cushion, and both dance and sing, "Prinkum, prankum is a fine dance (9). Afterwards the woman takes the cushion as the man did.

It is only of late years that quadrilles and waltzes have been danced in our neighbourhood by the working classes, but, as we have seen, foreign and Court dances have from time to time in the past become naturalized in our village dancing, so no doubt it will be in the future.

SPORTS AND GAMES.

Our old villagers often tell us that there are no sports now to be compared with those that went on in their young days. But of course, they look back to the days before machinery invaded the fields. You cannot have amusement without people to be amused.

84

It was inevitable that the recreations of the people should change with those other changes that have, to so great an extent, taken the life and joy from our country districts.

But there was one feature in our old country sports that is very valuable. They were the pastimes of the people as a community, in their own villages; although sometimes creating enthusiasm over a wide district. The people, as a rule, originated and managed their own amusements, and did not require that they should be started and mainly supported by others.

The most popular and continuous of the old sports in our Glendale valley was the game of bowls, or "bools." It was wholly unlike the game of the same name which is so popular in Scotland. In principle it was more akin to golf. The course was a measured mile on the turnpike road, the usual playground of the people in those days. The "bool" was a round ball of metal, weighing about a pound and a half, but it was sometimes made of stone, by the players, to save the cost of iron and blacksmith's labour. It was thrown by hand along the course, and the object was to reach the goal with the fewest throws. There were two competitors in each game. The winner was the one who was first at the end of the mile course and first back again. In the ease of a tie the game was decided by a final round out.

The rules of the game were very precise, and each side took care that they were rigidly kept by their opponents. An impetus was gained by running about a dozen yards before throwing the "bool" It was hurled with great force, by swinging the arm below 'the shoulder, and at the same time springing up from the ground and alighting with one foot on each side. of a starting rod, which lay upon the ground to mark the beginning of the course. This rod was called the "Trigg," and was watched by a man called the "Trigger," who was able to recall the throw if the foot of the player touched the Trigg. After the first throw, the other throws were made at the exact spot where the "bool" rested. Each player was preceded along the course by an experienced "booler" on his own side in the game, who advised him as to the best spot at which to aim, so as to cover the greatest distance, and going on before he would stand at this spot, and raise a handkerchief on a stick, as a mark for the bowler.

One who took part in these contests says, "Many great matches were made in my time by eminent bowlers, their supporters attending in large numbers. . . . . The record match was between a man named James Grey, the champion bowler, and Thomas Rutherford, son of the village schoolmaster at Ford. He was a very fine man, tall and handsome, but not so fit to withstand fatigue as Grey, who was a spare man, very wiry and cool and several years older. Grey won both the out and return distances, so that the third trial was not required. The return match was played, and Grey was again successful."

On the last occasion of my visits I observed his tomb-stone, which showed his age at the time of his death to have been little short of ninety. Many miners from the local coal pits, which were then being worked, took part in this game, and a fight along the road was not infrequent."

It is probable that "booling" still exists as a game among the colliers of the Northumberland and Durham coal fields.

One would think, to hear the reminiscences of our villagers, that the time of their youth was an age of local champions. Besides the champion "booler," one hears much of Robert Nevins, or "Neve," the champion hammer "putter." He was one of Lord Tankerville's gamekeepers, and lived at Heaton Mill, on the Till, and is thus celebrated in the rhyme of Jack the Leash, our village weaver.

"They may come from Beaumont, the Tweed and the Till,
But they light in with their match at old Heaton Hill".

The rhyme may be poor, but there is in it an echo of the clannish feeling connected with the river valleys of the English border, and a record of that public spirit, emulation, and pride in local effort, which we could wish to see more of in the present day. The late Lord Tankerville once took Nevins to the Blair Athol games in which he greatly distinguished himself in hammer throwing. His prowess was also frequently shown at the games sometimes held at Etal under the patronage of Lord Frederick FitzClarence. The Etal games were for the most part like those of the present day, where country sports are held, and they included wrestling as a special feature. One who was an eye witness of these sports in the beautiful grounds of Etal Manor gives us a picturesque glimpse of the scene. There was a large house party, and among them the then Duchess of Roxburgh, who was walking about the sports grounds on the arm of

86

Lord FitzClarence, and with her closed parasol trying to prevent the fluttering breeze from showing too much of the white stocking, then so fashionable, made from the virgin cotton so fine sixty years ago, from South America. Among the spectators was Lady Haggerstone, and also Miss Peel, who was dark, tall and handsome, and wore to advantage one of those beautiful Paisley shawls, which have so entirely disappeared from the ken of the present generation.

Lord Frederick FitzClarence, Lord Tankerville of Chillingham and Sir Horace St. Paul of Ewart, were contemporaries and great lovers of sport. Lord FitzClarence encouraged local horse races, which were held on a peninsula formed by a bend in the river Till. This bend in the river, as seen from Crookham, appears in the exact form of a traditional shepherd's crook or a Bishop's pastoral staff, and there can be little doubt that from this, the village takes its name. The racecourse being so situated, the inhabitants on both sides of the river were able to witness the sport. In these races the farmers used to ride their own horses, and thus the interest of the agricultural inhabitants was mightily aroused, for the honour of the farm places was at stake, and there was plenty of material for the rhymes of Jack the Weaver, who recounted the names of the various horses and extolled the winners.

There are traditions among our people of the more cruel sport of cockfighting, common to all England at the time, and there are still with us those who speak, but with disgust, of badger baiting of which they were witnesses. The carted stag brought from Chillingham Park, where large herds still exist, was hunted by Lord Tankerville's stag hounds in the unenclosed common of our parish. Let us hope that the sport of otter hunting, of which so many of our friends do not at present see the harm, will before long, like these other cruel sports, pass away into oblivion.

St. Ninian's Fair.

Country fairs are, no doubt, all more or less alike, but sixty years ago they had an importance that they can never have again. Our fair was held neither in the village nor even within the boundaries of our parish, but in an open stubble field in a neighbouring parish, some distance from any dwelling, on the hill-side opposite the Cheviots. It seems to have no recorded history, but it was evidently at first established and held with that religious sanction that in ancient days was naturally given to the business as well as the innocent pleasures of men. It was called St Ninians' Fair. (10) The name takes us back to the very early days of Christianity in the North, for St. Ninian was the Apostle of the Picts circa 432. But it must not be supposed that our people speak the saint's name as it is spelt. With them it is "Trinian," the final "t" of saint only being retained to begin the name, and an "r" inserted to make the transition easy; just as St Audrey becomes "Taudry."

MOULDS FOR GINGER BREAD FAIRINGS.

The fair was held on the 27th of September. It was a great mart for sheep, cattle, and horses, and the sale of hardware, cooperage, and earthenware, but it is chiefly remembered as a pleasure fair. It was arranged as a street. On one side were the refreshment tents, kept by the publicans of the surrounding towns and villages, having the names of their signs on flags or streamers, and on the other side were stalls for the sale of sweets, finery, toys, and above all, the

88

gingerbread made in moulds to represent the Royal Arms, men, horses and dogs; these being par excellence, the "fairing" that was always expected by the young and old people who, for any reason, could not be present at the fair.

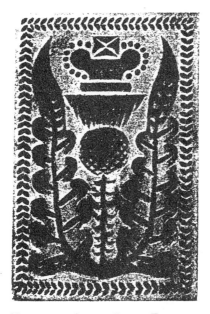

MOULDS FOR GINGER BREAD FAIRINGS.

There were also several games of chance going on that would not now be allowed. Thimblerigging was carried on by sharpers in the lanes and foot-paths leading to the fields, and another game called prick-the-garter. Good marble players were much attracted to a pile of about a dozen pennies to be shot at for a penny a shot, all the coins knocked down being the reward, The thoroughfare was filled from end to end with an animated moving crowd; cheap-jacks driving a brisk trade, travelling musicians, and ballad singers, who sold for a half-penny many an old song that doubtless had its origin in the folklore of the North.

89

Everyone went to the fair that could ride, drive or walk. It was an annual event to which young and old looked forward; and although no doubt there were evils connected with it, and its extinction by the rise of the cattle mart at the railway station is not to be regretted, the pity is that there is nothing that can take its place, and reproduce its good features as a social festival suited to the country.

(1) Mr. D. D. Dixon, of Rothbury, tells me that these six dances are not known in the Rothbury district of Northumberland.

(2) Dancing: Badminton Library, p.189.

(3) Sir George Grove's Dictionary of Music, vol. iv.

(4) Dancing: Badminton library, p.179.

(5) Dancing: Badminton Library, p.235.

(6) Sir George Grove's Dictionary of Music, vol. Iv.

(7) Whittingham Vale, by D. D. Dixon, p.68.

(8) Dancing: Badminton library, p.158.

(9) Dancing: Badminton Library, p. 159.

(10) Very distinct and interesting traces of our saint (St. Ninian) are to be found in the Northumberland parish of Wooler, - or, more strictly speaking, in that portion of it which is known as Fenton (a district which is now added to the parish of Doddington) a portion which, until the year 1313, constituted a separate parish, with its own church and graveyard. According to a local tradition it was here that St. Ninian began his preaching, and though of the church which doubtless bore his name nothing now remains but the foundations, there are yet, or were until very recently two abiding memorials of the saint, the one in the well called from him "St Ninian's Well" the other in the annual cattle fair, held on Sept. 27th (St Ninian's Day, O.S.), and popularly called St Ninian's Fair. - *Studies in Church Dedications* ii.,23 by F. Arnold Forster.

Chapter 12.

Border Customs

There seem to have been more curious customs connected with marriage than with any other social event, but nearly all of them have pased away. Courtship is not carried on openly as it is in the South, and even parents are kept in ignorance of an engagement until the banns are published. You may hear it stated that a certain couple are engaged, but from experience you hesitate to congratulate either party, lest you should give offence. You are not supposed to know, although you are perfectly aware of the fact.

On the evening before the marriage, there used to be a curious ceremony at the bride's house. Five or six of her girl friends would assemble, a tub of water would be brought, and they would wash her feet. During the operation a ring was dropped into the tub, and the young women would all plunge their hands into the soapy water, and the one who found it was the first, to be married.

There seems to have been a corresponding custom in the case of the bridegroom but this was more of a practical joke than a ceremony. It consisted of scrubbing the bridegroom if by any means he could be forced to submit to such rough usage.

The old custom of the "petting stick" is still sometimes observed n our weddings. The married couple, after coming from the church, find a crowd of men and lads assembled at the churchyard gate to make them pay toll before passing through. A bar of wood or a cord is held across the entrance. This the man always has to jump, but if he scatters money among the crowd it is let down for the bride to pass (1). In the old days, in case of refusal to pay, the bridegroom was ducked in a pond near the village, or at least compelled to walk through it. The bar placed across the gateway is called the "Petting stick." At Holy Island, where the custom is still observed, a stone in the churchyard serves the purpose.

On the north side of the Tweed there is the "Creeling" of the bridegroom. After the marriage ceremony, which is usually in the house of the bride's father, some men will come with an old "wood basket" or "creel," which is hung by a rope to the bridegroom's neck. It is then filled with stones until he can bear the weight no longer. He is only relieved when he stands a treat, or when, at the cost of being kissed by one of the creeling party, the bride cuts the cords and releases her husband. To make it difficult to cut the cords, wires are usually woven into them.

I am told by several of our people of a practice which they remember on the English Border somewhat like the foregoing, but it applied not to marriage but to jilting. A young man or woman who had been deserted by a sweetheart, and had taken up with someone else, had to undergo the penance of "swilling," that is, to be bonneted at the first opportunity with a "swill" or potato basket inverted and placed on the head. These customs certainly seem rough, inconsiderate, and even childish; but this rather goes to prove that they come down from a remote time.

In our village the bride on her return from church and before entering the house was made the subject of rather a pretty ceremony. A cake cut into small pieces was brought out on a plate and both cake and plate thrown over the bride's head, and it was thought the more lucky if the plate broke as it fell. This custom was observed about three years ago in our village and is likely to continue.

It is strange in these days to hear our old people refer to some of the customs of their younger days as things that were regarded as of so much more importance than is now given to them. An old widow remembers how much was thought of attendance of women at church for the churching service, which in the present day receives scant attention, or is altogether omitted. In the ancient "terriers" of our churches will be found an exact statement of the fee payable to the clergyman for performing this service, as a part of the income of his benefice. This, of course, represents the pair of turtle doves presented by Jewish mothers in the temple. How far a feeling of thanksgiving entered into the custom as it was followed seventy years ago in our district it is impossible to say, but it was carefully observed, and the social customs connected with it probably helped to secure its continuance.

In a household at the birth of each child a new cheese was provided, and a bottle of whisky wherewith to entertain callers. The baptism followed in due course. At the same time, or soon after, came the churching. The woman left her house carrying wrapped in paper a piece of bread and a slice of the cheese. The bread, if possible, was white wheaten bread, not the barley bread of the daily fare. This she carried to church As she went she was to give the bread and cheese to the first person she met. That person was considered peculiarly lucky, and had the privilege of buying a frock or the calico to make one, for the new-born child.

CUSTOMS CONNECTED WITH DEATH AND BURIAL

After a death it was a general custom to place a saucer containing salt on the breast of the deceased. The following is only related because it shows the hold this practice had on the minds of the people. Two men were waiting up for a farmer and his wife who were very late in returning from the market town. One of them became so tired that he lay down in a box bed and went to sleep. The other, by way of a grim joke, when his companion was slumbering heavily, arranged the bed as if a dead person were in it, and then, gently turning his friend on his back, placed a plate full of salt on his chest. Great was the anger of the man when he awoke with this awesome sign of death upon him.

The chamber of death is still for the most part draped with white, but a few years ago every article of furniture it contained was so draped. The clock was always stopped and its striking weight removed, and its face and that of any looking-glass (2) carefully hidden from view (3). No bright colour was allowed to be seen in the room.

The old fashion of wrapping the dead in a winding sheet has now quite gone. The last instance I knew of in my parish was at the hamlet of Heatherslaw. An old couple had lived there for many years. The wife died first, and in her coffin was stowed away an enormous length of very old hand-made linen, so old that it had become quite yellow. The Presbyterian minister who visited the house and saw the coffin before it was closed asked the meaning of so much linen being crowded into it, and suggested that it should be removed, but he was told that the old lady had hoarded the winding sheet for many years that she might be buried in it, and that there was another piece of linen of the same age and size laid up for the burial of her husband.

Some of our aged villagers have gruesome tales of the days of Burke and Hare. Two shearers who came to one of our farms for harvest work for some years, used to lodge at Burke's ill-omened

93

lodging house in Edinburgh, and although they sometimes had a good deal of money, which they had earned, about them, they never suspected any harm, and never suffered any loss. In one of our villages lived a family called McDougal. The father, mother and infant son happened to be staying in Glasgow. Burke, who was there at the time, became acquainted with them, the result being that the woman went off to Edinburgh with him, and deserted her husband and family. The father returned home to Crookham on foot, carrying his infant child in his arms.

It is with a shudder that those days are still referred to by those who remember them. Every churchyard had its watch house, and our villagers took their turn as watchers with cocked guns and pistols, ready for any emergency. It used to be one of the duties of the members of the local Burial Clubs to take their turn at watching. People were afraid to leave their houses after dark, a knock at the door was not answered unless it was known who was there, for there were tales of those who had been kidnapped and quickly carried off, their cries prevented by a plaster suddenly placed over the mouth. A village tradition asserts that a man who was a carter was one night coming up the hill by our church gate, when some men in the churchyard asked him to come and help them. They bound him to secrecy and he consented. He lived in the village and had been well acquainted with the man whose body was with his help dug up and taken away. The matter so burdened his conscience that he became melancholy it was said "he never looked up again," and did not live long afterwards.

One of the old sextons is said to have had a very unpleasant experience. He had lately filled in a grave after a funeral, but the soil being of soft clay, in a few days the mound sunk down to one side in an unusual manner. This attracted the notice if the friends of the departed, and their suspicions were aroused. It seemed evident to them that the grave had been tampered with. The sexton assured them that it was not so. He protested much, but could not content them, and so in self-defence he went through the labour of re-opening the grave. The coffin was opened and the corpse was found undisturbed.

After a funeral the near friend or relative of the deceased used sometimes to place a penny piece on the newly made grave just under the soil. By this means any disturbance of the grave was detected.

Two notorious body-snatchers were travelling in the coach between Alnwick and Wooler, having as their luggage two boxes whose contents may be imagined. As the coach neared Glanton, it was found to have been followed up by relatives of those persons whose bodies had been exhumed. When the coach reached Glanton the men were arrested and their prey delivered up. It is said also that one night a carriage containing, to all appearance, three men, drove up to the Blue Bell Inn on the road to Coldstream. Two of the men entered the inn for refreshment, the third remained sitting upright in the carriage: it was a dead body.

The prejudice that used to exist among the poor against hospitals and workhouses was partly due to the dread of dissection. But this prejudice has quite passed away. The subjects for dissection are those who are quite friendless or disowned and there are many such in the institutions of our large cities.

I have been many years rector of my parish, but only recently have discovered how many of my aged parishioners, and the fathers and mothers of others, were married, not in their parish church, but at a little inn on the Scotch side of the bridge which crosses the Tweed at Coldstream. There were three noted places on the Border for these marriages, Gretna Green, Lamberton Toll near Berwick, and Coldstream Bridge End, all situated on the main coach roads from London. But the Bridge End Inn at Coldstream was the nearest house over the Border in Scotland. The road which runs through Glendale and passes the foot of the Cheviots and Flodden Hill, must have often been enlivened by the post chaise of a run-away couple, and at an interval by another in hot pursuit containing an angry father or guardian. As one listens to an old man, who, when a boy, used to herd cattle by the road-side, one can almost hear the crack of the postillion's whip as he urges his horses along amid a cloud of dust, knowing well his reward if he can get safely across the bridge. The little cottage, now no longer an inn, has lately been restored by the owner of the Lennel estate; but it has been restored so carefully that it remains the same in effect as before, even to the water barrel near the door. The cottage as it fronts the road looks like a small one on the ground floor, but if you look down over the wall of the bridge you see that it, on one side at least, reaches down a considerable depth to the level of the river below, and rumour says it

95

contains, as an old pedlar expressed it, "several peculiar cellars. " Whether this implies that these were used as temporary refuges for runaway couples until the rage of the pursuer was overpast, I know not, but a glance at the nature of the building certainly suggests this to the imagination.

Of course it was the great difference between the English and the Scottish marriage law that led to these Border marriages. In England it was necessary to have banns called, with the condition of the residence of one of the parties during the time covered by the three Sundays of their publication, or else a licence, also involving residence. This, of course, necessitated delay, and a certain amount of publicity. Even an archbishop's licence was not to be immediately obtained, and was very costly, although it allowed greater latitude. But directly you crossed the Border into Scotland, marriages could be instantly effected. No residence was required, no questions were asked, the ceremony could take place in a house, a church, an inn, or in the open air. If a man and woman entered the Bridge End Inn it was only necessary for a witness to assert that he had heard the pair agree to be married, and the deed was done. But when this took place at the inn, a man who was jocularly called the priest was present, who declared the pair man and wife. If a young man and woman came in and the hostess said to the man, "Who is she?" and he answered, half in joke, "She's my wife," the marriage was supposed to be complete.

The first of these so-called "priests" was Patie Moodie, a shoemaker, the second, John Armstrong a mole catcher; the last man who regularly conducted these marriages and recorded them in writing was Willie Dickson, a shoemaker of Coldstream, an intelligent and fairly educated man. It seems that in his time the marriages were most frequent. He is said to have done a roaring trade, charging on average ten shillings and sixpence as his fee, but much more when "big gentlemen" and moneyed men required his services.

Some of these marriages were performed after this by a man called Laidler, a native of Wooler. He was deformed, and from the wheel-like motion of his legs and arms when walking, had the nickname of Row-Rumple. Brief certificates or "Marriage lines" were given to the newly-married couple, and duplicates of these were filed on a wire hung from the ceiling. Naturally, a great

96

number of these registers were lost. It is said that a man, whether in an official capacity or not is not stated, came from London and called at the inn for the express purpose of securing the registers of marriages that had taken place there. He offered to pay heavily for them. The innkeeper said he was sorry, but there had been "a bit of carelessness," and the papers had been thrown into the garden and burnt with other rubbish.

It is probable, however, that many of these certificates exist in the hands of private individuals. They would be of considerable interest if published. The marriages, although not solemnized, were valid by the law of Scotland.

CONTRACT OF MARRIAGE.

WE, J.M., residing in Wooler in the Parish of Wooler, and County of Northumberland, and Jane D., residing in Wooler and County of Northumberland, do hereby accept of each other as Husband and Wife, as witness our hands at Coldstream, this 24th day of March, 1850, before these witnesses,

and WILLIAM DICKSON.

KINGDOM OF SCOTLAND,
COLDSTREAM BRIDGE, PARISH OF COLDSTREAM,
COUNTY OF BERWICK.

THESE ARE TO CERTIFY, to all to whom these PRESENTS shall come, That..............................of the Parish of Cornhill, in the County of North Durham and..............................of the Parish of Kirknewton in the County of Northumberland having declared themselves Single Persons were MARRIED by me, agreeably to the Laws of Scotland, and after the manner of the Laws of the Church of England, this Sixth Day of October in the Year of our Lord One Thousand Eight hundred and Forty-two.

(Signed) WILLIAM Dickson.

This Marriage was solemnized between } us, and we hereby acknowledge ourselves as Husband and Wife. }

In the presence of { Robert Dickson } { Euphemia Jerdan } Witnesses

97

CERTIFICATES OF COLDSTREAM BRIDGE MARRIAGES.

THESE ARE TO CERTIFY that William Henderson and Ann Wilson both of the parish of Chillingham were married at Coldstream Bridge by mutual consent of each other as witness my hand this 17th of Oct. 1816.
Witness: John Hart.   WM. BURN.

These marriages were put an end to by an Act of Parliament, brought in by Lord Brougham, and passed in 1856, which required the Residence of one of the parties for a certain time before the marriage. Strange to say there is a persistent tradition in Coldstream that Lord Brougham himself was one of the "big gentlemen" who, knowing the laxity of Scotch Law took advantage of it and was married at the "Newcastle Arms" the principal inn at Coldstream, by the then "Priest," Patie Moodie, in 1819. The lady was Mary Ann, daughter of Thomas Eden, and widow of John Spalding. Lord Eldon is also said to have been married to Miss Surtees by Patie Moodie at the same place.

A former inhabitant of Coldstream, who unfortunately died leaving his letter unfinished, wrote me thus -

The books in my possession are only of the period covering April, 1844, to July, 1857, and are records only of the marriages so recorded. Witnesses' names appear over and over again at the different ceremonies, and they are all signed by William Dickson. The last date is. . . . . but includes a great number of your own and other parishes. There are no outstanding names of any particularly prominent people amongst the 3,500 odd marriages as recorded in Dickson's books, except one occasionally from County Middlesex, etc. On the other hand, the books bear evidence of having been tampered with, inasmuch as leaves here and there are missing, and in one case, a most deliberate and wilful obliteration has been attempted to blur the records of that ceremony.

These books have been of value to a good many Northumbrians in assisting them in their claims of legitimacy as heirs-at-law, and quite recently in a Glasgow Court, and also at Morpeth, were held as such.

As a boy, I remember my father taking with him a few friends of his own from Newcastle, and were shown the bedroom where proudly the host (Mr. Hume) pointed to the nuptial couch of the then Lord Brougham. No record of his marriage can now be obtained.

But it must not be supposed that those who crossed the Tweed in this way to get married were all rich fugitives from the South, hurrying along in coaches and chaises. By far the larger number of these marriages were those of our English Border folk, the working people of our villages and farmsteads. The simplicity and secrecy of these unions appealed to the reserved nature of the people who even now carry on their courtship, to use their own expression, "under hidlings" or in secret. The young people used to leave the village on foot, going out separately in the dusk of the evening, walking the eight miles and meeting at Coldstream Bridge, or at some appointed place along the road.

A young miner from our local colliery had for some time been courting Nan Allan, a young gipsy girl. At last they settled the day and decided to get married at Coldstream Bridge. So one Saturday evening they started to walk the eight miles together. It was considered a great event by all who knew of it, and the young couple were accompanied for some distance from the gipsy settlement by a crowd of friends, most of them miners. They had to descend a wide straight road over a steep hill. As they came near the foot of the "bank," they and the crowd behind them were brought to a sudden halt. The village carrier was on his way home from Berwick. He was a man of some character and authority among his neighbours. He saw at a glance what was going forward. Turning his horse and van across the road to bar the way he got down and told the young couple to go hack home, he would not allow any such doings. They must put up their banns and be married in the church in a proper way. One of the miners came up and seconded his efforts, telling the young man an invented story, that the first couple to be married in the church after its restoration, which had just been completed, would receive five pounds from the rector. This had great weight with the young fellow, who was far from strong minded. The would-he bride was naturally very much distressed and strongly urged the young man to carry out his intentions. However, the counsels of friends prevailed, the pair were saved their long walk, and the banns were read on Sunday in the church. Sad to say, the young man proved faithless. Probably he found out that the story of the five pounds was a fiction. He withdrew the banns, and some time after he married another woman.

Our country fairs were in those days responsible for many of

99

these Border marriages. Each year several young couples, after spending the day at the fair, would go off to Coldstream in the evening and get married. This was very much the custom with young people belonging to the families of our coal miners. The clergy of our parishes and the ministers of Presbyterian churches did their utmost to check what indeed was widespread disregard of the sanctity of marriage; for, apart from the fact that there was no religious ceremony, these marriages were disgraceful affairs, whisky entering largely into the proceeding. Many a time did the old rector here insist on marrying in the parish church with all due solemnity, and after a severe admonition, those of his people who had eluded his vigilance and been, as they termed it, "buckled up" at Coldstream Bridge.

Sad stories are told of the heart-burnings of many of those who returned from these hastily contracted unions, for there was but little romance about most of them. There were some that hid tragic endings. There is a spot on the road to Coldstream which bears the name of Ghostly Cut. It is a deep cutting through which the road passes, just before you come in sight of the Cornhill railway station. It is asserted that there, appears at times the spirit of a bride, who was returning from her Coldstream Bridge marriage with her husband, when the carriage came into collision with some carts, and she was thrown out and instantly killed. If we only knew one half of the incidents that have given a name to our Brides Braes and Ghostly Cuts what a volume of tragedies we should have.

(1) May not this be a vestige of the old Roman custom on the homecoming of the bride, who, wearing a long white robe with purple fringe. a bright yellow (flammeum) veil and shoes of the same colour, was led in procession to her future home. As she approached, she was welcomed by the chorus and lifted over the threshold.
"Transfer omine cum bono
Limen aureolos pedes." --- *Catullus*, LXI., 166-7.

(2) In Germany, England, Scotland and other places as far off as India and Madagascar it is still believed that, if after death a person sees his image reflected in a mirror in the same room as the dead, he will shortly die himself; hence in many places it is customary to

100

cover up looking-glasses in a death chamber."--- Elworthy, *The Evil Eye*.

(3) In Oldenburg it is thought that if a person sees his own image after a death, he will die himself. So all the mirrors in the house are covered up with white cloth. In some parts of Germany and Belgium after a death not only the mirrors but everything in the room that shines or glitters (windows, clocks, etc.) is covered up, doubtless because they might reflect a person's image.--- Frazer's *Golden Bough*, vol. I., p.294.

Chapter XIII

Superstitions

A great many of our people still keep a pig, generally those who are the most thrifty and industrious. The killing of the pig is an important event, and something of a social function. There is a tea party of neighbours, and the best cake is baked. Portions of the meat, especially of the spare rib, are sent as presents to particular friends. The pig is never killed during a waning moon. The moon must be either increasing or full. This the people are most careful about.

There can be little doubt that we have in this the remains of a most ancient superstition. Mr. Elworthy says in his book on the *Evil Eye*, p. 333, "the pig was sacred to Demeter and came at length to be an embodiment of the corn goddess herself." He also mentions that Herodotus says, "it was unlawful to sacrifice the pig to any gods but to the moon and Bacchus, and then only at full moon." I was told the other day by an elderly woman, living at one of our farms, that she remembered that "herds," old men, went by the moon: "they wad'na kill a pig to anybody if the moon was'na right". At another farm I was told that a former tenant of the farm would not allow the people to kill their pigs when the moon was "going back," because, if this were done, the bacon would not cure, or else would "crine," or shrink in cooking. If killed in the "back-going moon" the meat would "boil in" instead of "boiling out." It is the universal practice, at the farm cottages at least, to hang up the pig's head on a nail near the house door with its face outwards. The Holy Island fishermen will never keep a pig at their homes, nor will they ever mention the word pig. (1) They call it "the animal" or "the article." They will not go out to sea if they have met a pig or a hare, or a flat-footed person on the same day.

It is thought unlucky for a hare to cross your path or come running towards you. Witches were able to conceal their identity by taking the form of hares. I am told that in the village of Fosbury in Wiltshire an old woman died some twenty years ago who was firmly believed to have had the power of injury as a witch. One day the baker was coming from the Manor and she asked him for a lift, but as he refused, she is said to have taken off the wheels of his cart.

She was also reputed to have the power of turning herself into a hare. One day in this disguise the harriers pursued her, and as she was taking refuge in her cottage a farmer shot her in the back. The next day the doctor was sent for to the cottage and found a wound in the old woman's back (2). A hare's foot was evidently used as a charm against witches, as they are often to be found nailed outside a door

Curtseying to the moon is a custom still observed. In the South of England the number of curtseys must be either three or nine Turning money in your pocket on seeing the new moon for the first time also prevails, and here, as in other parts of England it is unlucky to see the new moon for the first time through glass. The window must be opened if you happen to be indoors and you must not look through spectacles.

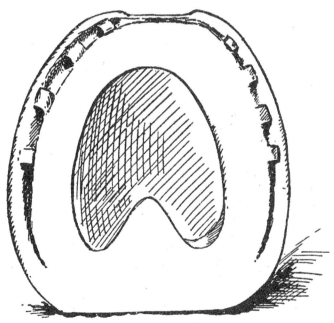

ROUND HORSE SHOE

It is believed that when you hear the cuckoo first, if you are at the moment standing on hard ground you will have a season of hardship and hard work, but if on soft ground, an easy time, "a fine growing year." It is unlucky to see a lamb for the first time in the season if its back is towards you, lucky if it stands facing you.. The horse shoe is with us the charm most generally used against evil entering the house. There are few doorways without one, or more, hanging on a nail or amongst the woodbine or other creeping plants. The horse-shoe should, strictly speaking, be hung inside the door. The round horse-shoe is considered the most efficacious. Is this the full moon? It is curious how persistent this custom is; even those who are the most free from superstition continue it, and it will probably last as long as the idea that it is unlucky to spill salt, and that this ill-luck may be avoided by throwing a pinch of it over your left shoulder.

WITCH'S STONE.

It was considered a most effectual defence against witch-craft to have what is called a witch's stone, hung inside the doors of cottages and cow byres. The cow, being the most valuable possession of the cottager "seems to have been everywhere the most susceptible to this malign influence. One of these stones used to be hung to the door of every cow byre" and most of the cottages. Within the last two years I have known of three families still retaining this custom. In one case the stone was taken from the door and presented to me.

On my hesitating to take what was considered a charm against ill-luck the woman of the house said, "Oh, but I have a Rowan branch and that will do instead."

These stones were found in the fields, in the river, or by the sea-side, and their peculiarity is that they have holes naturally formed in them, and so are comparatively rare. The string by which they are hung from the inside of the door is threaded through these holes. Brockett (3) calls these "Adder Stones" because the perforations are supposed to be made by the tongue of an adder.

A kind friend sends me the following curious reminiscence concerning the use of the Rowan tree (Mountain Ash or Quicken tree) as a defensive charm:--- "Some fifty-eight years ago as I was standing at the door of a farm-house, on the road a few miles from Sheffield, I observed a man approaching carrying on his shoulder, well poised, a sheaf of stout sticks cut in about even lengths. He seemed a strong man, aged about fifty, but the weight of his load seemed somewhat burdensome to him. The mistress of the house, and one or two more, seeing me looking curiously at him, laughed, and I asked the reason. I was told that the man was sane on all points save one, the fear of witches; and that when leaving home to go some distance, he fortified himself against their machinations by carrying this heavy load of Rowan tree boughs. This incident was impressed upon my mind by the savage look he gave me on seeing me laugh. He halted one moment to utter a, curse and then went on his way."

The Rowan was in our district constantly used as a charm against witchcraft, and was believed to be a certain aid to the dairymaid when the butter refused to "come." Butter churning is known to be a "kittle" thing, but the Rowan surely counteracts the evil influence that prevents the butter "coming." The cow was protected by a branch of the Rowan tree tied to her horns.

When a cow was "witched" it was the custom to put salt on her back. She was sometimes sold to a neighbour, the money being passed from hand to hand over the cow's back. This seems invariably to have been successful.

February 26th, 1907. An old man of 89 tells me that he knew a woman who had a cow which for some reason gave milk but no cream. She had a friend who came to see her, and who, on being told of the circumstance, said, "I will buy the cow of you; let me pass a sixpence to you over the cow's back in payment and all will be right." This was done, and the desired effect was produced, the spell was removed, and henceforth there was rich cream in the milk.

A former parishioner writes that a householder of our village had a cow, and an old woman, who was accounted a witch, came one day for milk or butter. For some reason she was refused. Being angry she went out of the house saying that the family would "rue for it." No more was thought of this threat, but soon after, the cow became a complete shadow. One day she was being taken out to the field by her owner, and the old witch, who was passing by, turned and said, "Jimmy, there's far ower much light between that cow's legs." Then the man called to mind the old woman's threat. My informant adds, "I suppose if that woman had asked for the half of the man's house after that, she would have got it; nevertheless, the cow died."

I have heard but little reference to fairies among the people. There are vague stories of men being pursued by fairies, who would ride on their horses behind them, or on the cart tail. Those over eighty tell me that in their young days grown up people and children believed that the fairies held their moonlight dances in an avenue of ash trees near the village, where there were well defined fairy rings in the soft turf, and aged people at that time were so convinced of the existence of these beings, that they would affirm that they had seen the dances going on, and that when a human being approached the fays would disappear. An old woman relates that in a field on a farm where she worked there was a deep hollow in the ground from which they said the fairies used to come, and the people at the farmhouse told her the fairies used to come to them from that place "to borrow a sieve to sift their corn."

"Ye canna' die wi' wild feathers." This remark came instantly when I enquired of a woman why it was that they never put pigeons' feathers into a pillow. She has the most absolute faith that pigeons' feathers, and, as a rule, game or wild feathers in a pillow prevent death coming on as it should, and cause it to be lingering and distressing. In this district pigeons' feathers are always carefully burnt, even by those who are not aware of the superstition which is the reason for the practice and which prevents their use.

But the idea that those who are on their deathbed cannot die easily on a bed or pillow of pigeons' feathers, is not peculiar to the

Border district. It. prevails in Hereford, and it exists in Surrey and probably in other places. The following extract from *Wuthering Heights*, by Emily and Anne Bronte is interesting in connection with this superstition. Of the distracted Catherine Linton we read -"
"A minute previously she was violent, supported on one arm, and could not help noticing my refusal to obey her. She seemed to find a childish diversion in pulling the feathers from the rents she had just made and ranging them on the sheet according to their different species; her mind strayed to other associations. 'That's a turkey's,' she murmured to herself, 'and this is a wild ducks; and this is a pigeon's. Ah, they put pigeons' feathers in the pillows; no wonder I couldn't die; let me take care to throw it on the floor when I lie down.'"

I was visiting a woman at a farm in my parish. She told me that a relation of hers was once nursing an old man in a parish not far off who was very ill and "couldn't die." The family were most anxious to ascertain the reason. Someone suggested that perhaps there were pigeons' feathers in his pillow. The pillow was carefully examined and did not contain any. The case was then thought still more serious, and it was suggested that something must be on the old man's mind, and it was decided, to send for the parson. When the vicar came he questioned the man closely to find out what it was that was troubling him. Concluding that it was a case of possession by Satan, he tried to exorcise the evil spirit, making passes over the man and exclaiming "Avaunt ye," and "Aroint ye," but without avail. The old man still "could not die," and was very miserable on that account. All at once he beckoned the clergyman to come very near to him and whispered in his ear, "I have five daughters, and none of them have been christened, and Almighty God won't let me die until it is done." So the clergyman faithfully promised to perform the baptism of his children, and he was able to die.

It was this curious narrative that first called my attention to the superstition concerning pigeons' feathers, and it surprised me to find it so generally held.

There is on the road from Wooler to Kirknewton, on a farm called New Yeavering, a small wood by the roadside, called the March Plantain, from the fact that it is the boundary between that farm and Akeld. The steward of New Yeavering was returning late on the evening of Christmas Day 1904, after attending at Wooler a

107

religious service of the Plymouth Brethren, of which body he is a member. On reaching a field on the farm near the Plantation he heard the heavy galloping of a horse coming towards him in a field on his right-hand side. It stopped suddenly when it, reached the hedge, and snorting, put its head over the hedge, and a rider was seen to be on its back. It was white and so was its rider.˙ It then turned and galloped heavily away, as it had come, and disappeared in the field. The steward went at once to his farm stable and found all his horses there. There was no white horse on the farm. I have since found from enquiry of two families who are unknown to one another, and who had both lived at different times at the adjoining farm of Old Yeavering, that the March Plantain was always known to be haunted, and children were afraid when passing it.

Every road and lane no doubt has its tragedy. A young man was once walking towards Cornhill-on-Tweed to visit his sweetheart. On the way he saw someone seated on the wall of a small bridge by the wayside. He went towards the figure and was astonished to find it was the girl he was hastening to visit, but the figure vanished as he looked at it. He went on, and reaching the house, found his sweetheart dying of a sudden illness.

The former vicar of a neighbouring parish declared to me that the first night he came to his new vicarage he saw the ghost of his predecessor standing at the foot of his bed and looking intently at him.

A lady relates the following experience. "When I was a girl of eleven, I lived at C. . . . One afternoon in winter I went into the church to fetch some books for the choir, of which I was a member. On entering the church I saw the vestry door on the north side of the chancel slowly opening. A figure appeared to glide around the door. It gave me the idea of some evil being. It was a tall figure draped in black, with long fringes across the breast from shoulder to shoulder. Over the head was a sort of cowl, also black, fringed along its front edge. The face was long, with pointed chin, and with two pointed upper teeth showing in contrast, to a black face. The hands were black, one hand gripping the fringe across the chest. The face looked intently at me, with coal black eyes. I was struck with horror, dropped the basket, and ran home, my heart beating horribly. This happened many years ago, but the appearance so imprinted itself on my memory, that I see it as distinctly now as I did at the time. My sister, who was older than myself, saw the same apparition in the same place, a fortnight after this, and was as much terrified as I was, running home breathless. When my sister saw the figure it was standing behind the reading desk."

December 25th, 1906. I heard today the following account of what really seems like a genuine case of telepathic communication from the dying to the living. It was told me by the nephew of the woman who died. He said: "You will remember that my father's sister died lately in Peebles. She had not been ill, but died suddenly; in fact, to the surprise of her family, she was found dead in her bed. Well, in the early morning of the day, Mother dreamt that she was coming towards the door of our house, and as she was passing the water barrel, she felt something pluck at her arm. Before she reached the door, she felt the same thing again, but when she entered the door a full hand was laid on her arm, and she saw the face of her sister-in-law, which vanished into the house." This occurred at Ford to a farmer's widow. It was a dream, but it happened the very night of her sister-in-law's death, and it made a great impression on her.

It may be worth while to record a curious thing I was told by a cottager of this village. She said there used to be a stone built in at the back of her fireplace called an "aitch" (4) stone, but that when the fireplace was altered it was thrown away into the wood, where it still was. She said there was one of these stones in other cottages also. In the days of the Border raids the "aitch" stone, by emitting some peculiar sound, gave warning to the villagers of the approach of the raiders as they came across the Till over the bridge. The woman died soon after telling me this, so that I was unable to ask her more about it, but I have since heard the same thing from another resident in the village in connection with another of the oldest of the thatched cottages.

There is a farm not far south of Berwick on the London road which has the reputation of being haunted. Many years ago I heard from a woman who had lived there as a servant in the house, that she often saw her deceased mistress moving about the house in the day-time as when she was in the flesh. And now, from an entirely different source, I am told of the strange experience of a man and a boy who went to work at the same farm. They had to live in the farmhouse. The first night they arrived they had to sleep in a room which contained a mangle. To their horror, at a certain time in the night the mangle began to work of itself. It went on for two hours, working without any visible hand touching it. The man and his son found from the other inmates of the place that this was a frequent occurrence, so much so that it was regarded with indifference by those who knew about it, but was not talked of outside.

In the farm village of Kimmerston there lived a woman who was reputed to be a witch. One twelfth of May a shepherd, who was leaving the farm, was all ready for the "flitting," with his carts packed with the household plenishings. As was usual on these occasions, he had said farewell to his fellow servants, who had met by invitation at his house to take some refreshment and wish him good luck. Unfortunately he had not invited a poor woman, who was suspected of possessing the evil eye; so that when all was ready for the start, both horses absolutely refused to move. How the people came to the conclusion that this was caused by the witch in revenge for not being bidden to the farewell function, is not stated, but they did come to this conclusion. She was at once invited to the house to partake of the good cheer; the horses then freed from the spell, started willingly with their loads.

In one of our villages named Crookham there lingers still the memory of a strange incident that occurred some sixty-five years ago. In spite of the length of time since its occurrence, and a certain want of evidence in the matter of time and the sequence of events, it seems quite worthy of record, and I cannot help thinking it to have been a genuine instance of "projection" or second sight, as a warning before death.

I first heard the story many years ago from a dweller in the village, but all I can remember of what he said is that there was a cart accident, and two men were killed when nearing the place, as they were returning home from Wooler in the evening; but on the same day one of them was seen walking about the village.

Now, this story I had quite forgotten, until reminded of it by a passage in a letter I lately received from a friend in London, who was the Church of England schoolmaster at Crookham at the time. He says some sixty-five years ago he was standing at the window of the boys' schoolroom, which is now the parlour of a cottage, and looking out, saw a man in his work-day clothing hoeing between rows of potatoes, the haulms of which had grown up high. He knew the man well, and was going out to speak to him, but was delayed a few moments by something in the school. On turning round again to look out, the man was not there. It is evident that the man's sudden disappearance impressed him, for he goes on to say, "I thought when I got home that the man might have fallen in a fit and been hidden from view by the tall haulms. Next morning I mentioned the matter to two or three other persons on entering the hamlet. I found that the man I had seen the day before among the potatoes had gone to Wooler that day with his father-in-law on business. Late at night they had not returned home. Their friends set out to see what had become of them. A short distance along the road they found the cart overturned, and both the occupants dead. My view of the son-in-law was not a casual glance, but of three or four minutes' duration at least."

On receiving this account from my friend I called on James Nevins of Crookham, a man advanced in years, but with an excellent memory. I asked him whether he had ever heard of a cart accident in which two men of the place had been killed. He knew about the accident, mentioned the names of the two men, Logan and Tyndall, and told me that the latter, the son-in-law of Logan, was found lying dead under the cart. I asked whether there was anything strange in connection with the affair. "Well," he said, "the young man's money had been taken from him". "But," said I, "was there not something else that was talked of at the time?" "There was," he said. "Now, what was the man's name that saw him! Aaron Thompson, yes, it was Aaron that saw him. Aaron was working in the allotment field, and he looked up, and there was Tindall coming towards him; he went on with his work for a minute thinking to have a 'crack' with him, for the two were intimate friends, but on looking up Tindall had disappeared. He was so surprised that he left his work and went some distance towards the slope of the hill to look for him."

I have not been able to get any evidence as to the time of these two distinct appearances of the same man to two different people at different spots, but they were previous to the man's death; the appearance to Aaron Thompson so far as I can ascertain, was some days before death. The impression left on the minds of the two who saw the apparition seems to have been in the one case, anxiety, and

111

in the other case, extreme surprise at the man's sudden disappearance. The allotment field where the appearance to Aaron Thompson took place is not anywhere near the potato field in which the man was seen by the schoolmaster.

(1) When he hears the unlucky word "pig" mentioned, a Scotch fisherman will feel for the nails in his boots and mutter "cold airn." The same magic words are even whispered in the churches of Scotch fishing villages when the clergyman reads the passage about the Gadarene swine.---Frazer's *Golden Bough*, vol. I p.349.
It is particularly unlucky to utter the word "sow," or swine," or "pig while the line is being baited; if anyone is foolish enough to do so, the line is sure to be lost.-Frazer's *Golden Bough*, vol. I., p.453.

(2) Frazer gives instances from many parts of the world of 'A belief in the possibility of a man possessing an *alter ego* in the form of some animal' ---*Golden Bough*, vol. III, p.408.

(3) In his *Glossary of North Country Words.*

(4) I have spelt the word as I heard it pronounced, but probably the right word is echo.

Chapter XIV.

Contraband.

The romance of the Border land changes its character, but does not pass away. After the greater conflicts between England and Scotland, culminating in Flodden Field, came the lesser Border raids, and the vengeance of tribal feuds, and then, in more settled times owing to unequal laws in the two countries, the romance of smuggling set in; brides were with as much fear and trembling smuggled northwards across the Border, as casks and bottles of whisky were deftly made to elude the vigilance of the exciseman southward. It may not be strictly correct to apply the term romance to contraband trading, but if love and war have always afforded abundance of adventures, so also, both in fact and fiction, have the illicit still and the clever but dishonest evasion of the duty on excisable goods been fruitful in incidents full of variety and excitement. Seventy years ago there were but few constables, but our principal roads were patrolled by a number of excisemen. They were well mounted, and armed with pistols. Their names are still familiar to our old people. Their chief duty was to prevent the smuggling of untaxed whisky from Scotland to England, and to prevent its manufacture in secret stills south of the Border. At that time the law did not allow less than eighty gallons at a time to be brought across the Tweed. A bottle of whisky could be bought in Coldstream for eighteenpence, just one half what it would cost in England. No wonder, then, that smuggling it over the Border was a constant and general practice. The law forbidding it, and the ever present show of force in the Excise officers, only acted as a stimulus to ingenuity and daring, in a people inheriting much of the caution and reserve of the Borderers of old. As far as one can gather from the traditions of the district, not only were the poor concerned in this business, but nearly the whole countryside was in a conspiracy to get their whisky cheap and evade the law, many of the farmers being regularly supplied. One of these, it is said, succeeded in bringing a cask of whisky home, but found the officers awaiting him. He could make no excuse for himself, but with unutterable meanness mentioned the name of the firm which supplied it, and who had to pay a fine of several hundred pounds.

It was often the practice to conceal bottles of smuggled whisky in the corn stacks. One day a farmer was entertaining a cattle-dealer. As is the custom, he first, as the host, helped himself to a glass of whisky, and then finding there was not enough for his guest, went out to fetch another bottle from the corn stack. His guest on taking it made a wry face, much to the chagrin of the farmer. This and all the other bottles in the stack had been emptied by the farm hands and filled with water.

In another instance bottles were safely hidden in the wall of a sunk fence, the long grass which fell over the edge concealing them. There is a story of a dog called Caesar, who was a great smuggler. He was a terrier of the Dandie Dinmont breed, a long bodied dog with short legs. He had been trained to carry from Coldstream a bundle containing one bottle of whisky. When tired he would lie down, carefully guarding his burden; probably the excisemen knew the trick, but wisely allowed Caesar to pursue his journey.

There lived in Coldstream in those days a worthy minister named Thomson. He was well known, because he obtained a licence to print Bibles which was then in Scotland, as it is now in England, a special privilege. These Bibles he used to sell in a wide district on both sides of the Tweed. He had as a servant and coachman an ex-soldier. This man carried on a very different trade, and for a time a very safe one, whenever his master drove into England. He not only packed his master's Bibles in the trap, but always managed to put in with them a package of his own, which he very easily disposed of as his master made his round of visits. But this sort of thing had its natural termination. The story goes that poor Mr. Thomson was prosecuted as a smuggler, although, no doubt, perfectly innocent of the crime.

An inhabitant of a neighbouring village, now ninety years of age, tells me that he smuggled whisky himself. Obtaining it at Coldstream he poured it into a bladder which he had placed in his tall hat and wore sedately home, a distance of six miles. He was, he said, always greatly relieved when he had run the gauntlet of the Excise officers, two of whom lodged in a house in the main street of Cornhill-on-Tweed.

Much smuggling in a small way was done by women, who wore tin cases made to fit around the body beneath their clothes. These cases had a hinge at the back and were fastened in front with clasps,

114

and had a small tap on the left side.

When returning from visiting friends or shopping on the Scotch side, our English folk used very generally to bring home the forbidden spirit concealed in bundles or under their purchased goods.

A kind friend, now advanced in years and a native of our countryside, gives the following reminiscences on this subject:---

"I have also met men carrying soft ware packs, such as cloth, hosiery, etc., having bottles or small kegs of whisky bedded therein, which they sold when opportunity offered. I remember meeting a hawker in the daytime on a field footpath carrying a pack, the outer covering being of stout hempen material and held together by leather straps. I asked him for a glass of whisky; he scanned me for a few seconds with a keen searching eye, and then undid the straps, and, taking out a small keg and glass, supplied me, and asked for threepence, and strapping his pack again, passed on. On another occasion, I met a man, whom I knew, near Ilderton, who asked me if I could pay for a glass of whisky as he had no money upon him, and there being no inn near, he led me across half a mile or more of rough country to a low cottage tenanted by an old woman and her daughter, to whom I could see he was known. He gave a nod and sat down. The window faced the back-garden, and I observed the daughter go to the garden wall and take off a cope-stone, and thrusting her arm deeply down, bring up a bottle from which she served whisky. I was then about sixteen years of age."

"There was a deep well in a small wood opposite the Toll-bar at Ford Bridge on the left approaching from the village. When boys, we played in the wood, and tried to plumb it by tying a string round a stone and dropping it in. On one occasion cords were seen suspended from hooks on big nails driven into the sides, at a depth of a foot or so under the surface of the water; on drawing them up, bottles of whisky were attached to them. The proximity of the well to the toll-bar suggests the reason of their being there. The toll-gate was always kept locked during night time, and the' toll-keepers had to turn out and open it to let every vehicle pass without delay. Now, at that time, some 65 years ago, the night traffic of carts across the Till was large. Scotch farmers then used great quantities of 'clot' lime as manure, which was procured at the Lowick kilns, and as comers were served in order of arrival, night traffic was great in order to get to the kilns early. Benighted foot-travellers also would find this a pilgrim's rest as other roads come together at the point. The retail dealers got their supplies from bulk smugglers who crossed the Border, and from illicit distilleries on the English side and the apprehension of the former and detection of the latter gave anxious occupation to the Excise staff.

"Illicit stills were in operation in various places on the northern part of the country. There was one in Chiptain's Dene, about half a mile north of Hay farm in a deep secluded part, in a cave, and was in active work during night only so that smoke might not be seen and when not in operation the 'worm' was taken away and hidden. Some boys from Hay farm attended Ford School, and I recollect hearing them talking about the 'worm' having been found by someone living in the neighbourhood, but not interfered with. Country folk seldom helped the Excise

"There was a still near Wooler, carried on by a man called Richardson whom I knew when a boy, and had opportunities of hearing his wife, who assisted him, talking much about it. At that time there lived at Wooler a man called 'Blind Willie the Fiddler,' who with another notorious smuggler named Dover, who hailed from Lowick, worked the Cheviot district on horseback. On one occasion they were encountered by two Excise officers, and after a struggle made good their escape, but Dover received a pistol shot in the heel."

The name of the smuggler one hears most of in our part of the border is that of Philip Wallace, who lived at Etal. This was evidently a very daring character, and owing to his cleverness, seems never to have been captured with sufficient evidence against him. He owned a horse which always outstripped his pursuers. He had a still not only at Chiptain's Dene, between Ford and Etal, but also on Ford Common and at Lowick Mill. He found the disused shafts, and adits of the local collieries, and the thick whin bushes of the common, very well adapted for his nefarious trade, and the storage of his kegs of spirit when ready for his customers. It is surprising to find, that with such a strong cordon of mounted Excise officers watching the Border, the smuggling and the manufacture and sale of whisky should have been carried out with such impunity. But the people must very generally have connived at it. The nature, too, of the country, with its wide moorlands and the proximity of the Cheviots to the long Border line, were favourable to the free traders. They knew all the most secret tracks among the moors and hills far better than the excisemen. And the smugglers could find no better depots for their goods than the secluded valleys and recesses of the Cheviots.

Besides the bringing in of untaxed whisky from Scotland, there was in our part of Northumberland a considerable trade in gin from Holland. It was bought from the smugglers on the coast and concealed in large quantities in corn stacks, and even in dung heaps.

A man would be working in a turnip field, the Excise officers come up to him and say, "You must come with us." He replies, "I have no time." They say, "You must come, my friend, and bring your horse and cart"; he unwillingly obeys, and is led by them to a farm yard where a heap of straw is found covering quite a load of small kegs in which rum and gin was conveyed. These kegs were slung over the horse's back and could easily be removed and hidden. The poor man whose cart was summarily requisitioned, not being himself implicated, is ultimately sent home with a present of the spirit.

Boulmer, near Long Houghton (pronounced Boomer), on our coast was a place noted as a hold for smugglers of gin from Holland. There was at that time no regular coast-guard service. There is still extant a doggerel rhyme which says---

"Jimmy Turner, of Ford, did not think it a sin,
To saddle his horse on a Sunday and ride to Boulmer for gin."

The traditions of smuggling from the coast inland have almost faded from the memory even of our oldest people. But they remember the days of dear salt, and the fear of the salt officer. Salt was then tenpence a "forpit," and it was a matter of anxiety to provide enough to cure the pig and to lay down the butter for the winter. Colliers' cottage doors were left unlatched all night, as they came in at all hours from the local pit. A man suddenly enters the house, to the alarm of the family who are in bed. He says, "I will not hurt a hair of your head if you will just let me stay a while, for the Excise officer is after me." He was smuggling salt.

Referring to those days a friend sends me the following note When a little boy I can remember a woman of the villa coming into our house after dark, and with bated breath saying, "He has come," and leaving instantly to tell others that the salt man had arrived. He brought his sacks to the cottage of a tall gaunt Scotch woman named Jeannie Macdonald, a widow, and I heard that he had sold out his stock and gone early that morning."

The salt brought in bulk was retailed by women, who carried it in sacks on their backs. On the rare occasions when the exciseman found them selling it and they tried to escape he would, on coming up with them, cut the sack with a knife and allow its contents to

117

flow out.

Those who smuggled spirits or salt in bulk did not travel more than they could help by the high road, but across country and by the most secret and unfrequented tracks.

There is a path among the hills by Newton Tors called "Salter's Path" to this day.

One can hardly believe that within the memory of those living in our midst, the state of things should have existed which such incidents disclose.

Chapter XV.

Words and Names

A favourite subject with our old people when they have a "crack" with the priest is the "schooling" and schoolmasters of their youth. They carry you back to the days when education was a scarce thing among the poor. They tell you how their parents strove to pay for it out of their slender wages, and how hard it was to do this when the family was large, and it was difficult to provide even barley bread for the household.

With all due allowance for the defects of failing memory in our aged friends, and their dim retrospect of many years, we cannot help feeling that the old village schoolmasters they describe with unbounded enthusiasm, were very fine men indeed, and true teachers.

With them religion held always the foremost place, and the Bible was the chief text-book used. There were few secular subjects taught then, but in those subjects the scholars were thoroughly well grounded. Technical instruction was not neglected, and boys were taken out to learn land surveying, and the measurement of wood and stone. The old foolscap "count" books into which the school work was carefully copied show that geometry was sometimes also taught to elder boys. One of these schoolmasters in particular is well remembered, and a dozen times in the course of many years have I met those of our migratory people who attended his school, and were still full of admiration for him. He was a Mr. Hewit, a clergyman of the Church of England, and vicar of the parish of Ancroft. Feeling the need of instruction for the young of his parish, he took the matter in hand himself, and laboured for many years as master of the village school. His loving and self-denying work was greatly valued by his people, and is even now spoken of with the greatest gratitude and respect.

We cannot, fairly compare the old country schools with the new. I merely allude to the matter of education as connected with the language of our people. To my knowledge, thirty years has made a great change in the way they talk. It is inevitable that in our modern school the children must soon cease to talk in the same way as their parents and grandparents. It has not become so yet. In the

119

playground and the house the border tongue still holds its own, and if you are fresh from the South, and overhear the children at their play, you will not understand them. We do not like old landmarks to be done away: the old tree that has taken centuries to grow, and which is, when we think of it, beyond all contradiction the finest plant in the garden, we hesitate to remove, even when it seems necessary to do so. It is the same with the ancient timbered house with its overhanging gables, telling us of a past age and simpler time than ours. We revere it, but it happens to stand in the modern street which must always be called, and always be, straight and so it must be sacrificed with all its traditions which never can be recalled.

Like the old tree and the old house so the old tongue of our people seems to be doomed in every part of our country. The educational machine pervades the land, even its remotest corners, and only concerns itself with crushing out individuality and bringing things to a dead level. Fine old words and expressions stamped with the history of the race, and used by the village children in their homes and in their play are, of course, never heard in the schoolroom. There, the tongue of master and scholars is that of the most modern English historical or geographical reader. There is just one practice which saves many of the old words, and that is the reading of the Bible and Prayer Book, and this is grudgingly allowed in the modern syllabus. Of course, the time must come for local words and dialects to pass away, but let us treasure them as long as we can. Instead of stamping them as vulgarisms, let the schoolmaster take note of them, and as occasion may arise, point out to the children their history as far as it is known. At least let the old words find a place in the school museum, side by side with the flint arrow heads and axes.

To begin then with a word dear to our school children, and used chiefly at their outdoor treats. The swing, which always attracts a little crowd of them even when the rest are occupied with other games, is to them the "shuggy," a word perhaps more expressive than beautiful, but likely to live on as long as our children love the thing which it describes. At the feast which begins the treat it is the "spice loaf" which is most conspicuous among the good things provided. The word cake is rarely used. The "spice loaf" of the baker is a quartern loaf or cake full of currants, and cut up into solid slices for the treats. The spice loaf of the cottage was a cake baked upon the girdle, also thick with currants, and called a "singing hinney".

It is a curious thing that our people always say "Butter and bread," "Cheese and bread," "Jam and bread," giving the staff of life the second place. The familiar blackberry which adorns our hedgerows with its graceful sprays, and in autumn with its richly coloured leaves, has no other name here but "bowowart." The children say, let us go and gather "bowowarts." The cow parsley which adorns our roadsides and gives so much lightness and grace to other flowers, when mixed with them, we call by the curious name of "Bad Man's Oatmeal." Bad man means the devil, and the small white flower of the plant certainly suggests the idea of meal, especially when its petals are shed upon the ground. The Bumble Bee is "bumla," distinctly Norse. The turkey cock, which looks so fierce, is called the "Bubbly Jock."

"Guizened" is a curious word applied to the shrinking of wood, especially the staves of a tub which has been standing for some time without water.

"My wife's tubby-kit is guizened," said one North country man to another to test his knowledge of the Border dialect. The "tubby kit" was a small wooden tub for washing.

"Thrifty" is a good old word. It is applied with us to the money box given to children to teach them the value of money. A child in our village was offered a threepenny piece for some small service he had done, but he declined saying, "Gie me a penny, I hae to put the siller in the 'Thrifty.'"

Several ancient words linger around the hearth, where you would naturally expect to find them. If you can manage to look up the chimney, the "lum," in an old cottage, you will see against the light the "wrangle tree," sometimes pronounced rannel tree. It is a stout wooden beam crossing the chimney about four feet above the fireplace, and built into the masonry at each end. Its purpose was to support by a chain passed around it the "crook" from which hung the kettle, pot, or girdle as required, at a convenient distance above the fire. The distance was easily regulated as the "crook" consisted of two flat rods of iron, one sliding on the other, and raised and lowered with a slot which fitted into a perpendicular chain of holes.

I have spoken of the "crook" in the past tense, as it is now almost upright bar working on a pivot above and below, on one side of the grate. It has a horizontal arm at right angles to it. From this arm hang three flat metal crooks of varying lengths. The whole thing sways over and away from the fire with its suspended kettles as may be required. Where the old "crook" remains it is hung from an iron bat lower down the chimney than the "wrangle tree." This ancient wooden balk was placed in the cottage chimney when iron was an expensive material. It was placed high up above the fire, but flames must have often reached it, and I know a cottage now where the housewife is very careful not to allow the fire to flame up too fiercely, lest it should become ignited and the house be endangered. I asked her how, with the beam so high up, the chain for the crook was put over it, and she told me that it used to be the duty of the sweep. The "wrangle tree" I understand, used to be a great obstacle to the climbing boys who, according to the cruel custom of the time, were sent up inside the chimnies to sweep them.

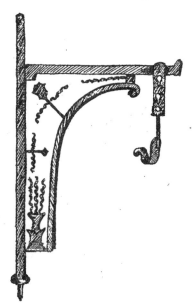

THE "SWEY."

122

"Reek," of course, is smoke; the latter word being rarely heard. Brockett has "reek-penny," a modus paid to the clergy in many parts of Northumberland and Durham for firewood. There was an ancient payment of this kind due to the rector of this parish, but long ago relinquished. The amount was fourpence for every chimney that smoked. The old friend who told me about the "wrangle tree" said that his mother used to sweep the chimney from outside. She would put on her husband's coat and climb up the "theaking" to the chimney, and put a long pole down to clean it. The thatcher is the "theaker."

February 28th, 1905. A thatcher who was son and grandson of a thatcher was working on a cottage roof in the village today. He told me that although rye straw was often used for thatching, wheat straw was the best and hardest. The thrashing machine breaks the straw and makes it less serviceable for thatching than it was when threshed with the flail. The neat bundles of wheat straw carefully combed and trimmed, and then called "reed," reserved for thatching, one never sees now. The flail beat chiefly on the heads of the corn and the stalks were left whole and strong, but now all passes through the thresher.

The thatcher told me that, in the very old cottages when first thatched, the roof consisted of about three horizontal rafters. Upon these were laid the branches of trees. Then the thatch was laid on and sewed to the branches with a needle. It is still tied to the rafters in the case of new work. I was very glad to find that this thatcher in finishing the ridge of the cottage roof, did not leave out the zig-zag ornament which seems such a constant tradition with thatchers, and adds just the necessary touch of lightness and finish to the work.

In our village about sixty years ago, although most of the houses were thatched with straw, heather roofing was used to some extent. It looked very neat when dressed with the thatcher's broad knife.

But we return again to the hearth. The other day the village postmistress told me that in her great grandmother's time, the supper dish of the family was "champit taties," consisting of mashed potatoes and sliced onions, cooked in a "yetling." The yetling was a round metal pot, with a bowed handle and three feet, like a gipsy kettle. The fashion then was for the members of the family to sit around the fire, each holding a spoon and a mug of milk, and to help themselves from the yetling which smoked upon the hearth. Plates themselves from the yetling which smoked upon the hearth. Plates and dishes, however were used at dinner.

The hinds' first meal before going out in the early morning was the "crowdie" It was quickly made with oatmeal and boiling water poured into it, and a little salt added. If not as digestible as porridge, it was warming during the early hours of labour and sufficed until breakfast time. There was also the "fat-crowdie," made in the same way, but with the addition of dripping, which is called "kitchen fee." The word "kitchen" still has the meaning of a delicacy of any kind, as an addition to ordinary fare: thus butter, jam, or cheese were "kitchen" to bread. The "fat-crowdie" is still eaten as a supper dish by some.

As one sits by the cottage hearth to have a friendly crack (talk) with its inmates, many an old word crops up which brings its story with it, and revives the memory of things and days gone by. The conversation chiefly turns on outdoor things. The wife tells one how, in her working days, all the women in harvest time went out "gathering" (gleaning), which was freely allowed by the farmer, and considered one of their most ancient rights by the poor. The little sheaves or handfuls that they gleaned were called "singles," the stalks being all neatly plaited together, this care showing how in those days every ear of corn was valued and treasured. And then when the "singles" were brought home the grain was "bittled" or beaten out by a sort of mallet called a "bittel" (1), against a large stone which stood at the cottage door. It is true that the poor have lost this privilege, but as corn is so much cheaper, and labour so much more valuable, they are able to look complacently at the machine which now rakes up every straw, and seems not to leave a single ear of grain among the stubble. They still glean in Essex, even after the machines have done their work.

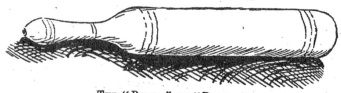

THE "BITTLE" OR "BEETLE."

In the days of gleaning it was often a substantial quantity of corn that was thus "bittled" out, and taken to the mill. It was no wonder that when corn passed as money for the hind's wages, and when every ear of wheat gleaned was a treasure, the miller was watched with a jealous eye, lest he should take too much of the meal or flour for his "mouter," in payment for the grinding. Many an ancient joke has been made at the miller's expense as to "moutering" the meal. People were lucky if they even got the sack in return for their hard earned corn. The word "mouter," so commonly used when wages were paid in corn, and when the vast water power of our country was employed to work our many riverside mills, now in ruins, has now, with the thing it represented, gone out of use, but it is still quite familiar to our aged people. The "mouter" was generally taken out of the meal, in handfuls by the miller's wife, and it was thought advantageous for the miller's wife to have a small hand.

The "ingle neuk" in our cottages has been pretty generally done away with. It was the cosy chimney corner, the space on each side of the fire, but under the wide arch of the chimney breast. This space is now taken up by the oven on one side, and the big pot on the other. Next to the "ingle neuk" for comfort and warmth was the "settle," or "sattle" as it used to be called; but this cosy seat with its arms and high back so effectual in keeping off draught, is now rarely seen, although the modern cottage is often more draughty than the old one that it replaces. It is a thousand pities that our workers are so fond of highly polished mahogany furniture, instead of keeping their "plenishings," which, if solid and homely, were comfortable and admirably suited to their position and use. Wherever a dresser remains with its full equipment of delft, or of willow pattern, or wild rose dishes and plates, large and small, is it not the envy of the rich lady, who how adores what is quaint and old-fashioned ?

The modern cottage inevitably does away with the old box beds which quite furnish one side of the old houses. In the spring-time one used to see many carts filled with sacks containing "kauf" (chaff), with which the beds were always stuffed. These beds, the people say, are soft and comfortable, and they have this advantage, that the old chaff is burnt and a new supply obtained each year.

The parson who has experience of parochial visiting will be careful, if possible, to avoid calling on the cottager on washing day.

careful, if possible, to avoid calling on the cottager on washing day. If he does venture in among the steam and washing tubs, he will probably hear from the woman of the house that she is "gey thrang," which is a very expressive way of saying she is very busy. In the days of one-roomed houses the term "thrang" was used of too many people in one bed. In our Border country that state of thing no longer exists, the landowners having, even in hard times, spent enormous sums in providing better houses for the farm labourers, and enlarging the old cottages of the villagers.

In winter, if you happen to be visiting a farm place in the evening at eight o'clock, you will hear a long blast from a cow's horn which answers the same purpose as the steam whistle of a factory; but it might be somewhat startling to a stranger, and might remind him of Robin Hood summoning his merry men in the ancient forests of England. This long-drawn note, sounding so weird in the darkness, is to call the hands who have just had their supper to go and "fettle" the horses. This means to feed and make them comfortable, and put all in good order for the night. To be in "good fettle" is to be in good form, *mens sana in corpore sano*. "What fettle?" is a usual question when acquaintances meet, and is equivalent to "How are you"? including the idea, How do you prosper? how goes it with you?

(1) The bittle, or beetle, was chiefly used for beating clothes after they were washed. It served the purpose of a mangle.

126

Chapter XVI

Words and Names

Among our weather signs perhaps the most noticeable is what is called here "upcast." It is that grand array of cumulus cloud which extends along a great portion of the horizon, in winter before snow, and in summer before a thunderstorm. When you see in a winter afternoon these grey masses of vapour rising from the North Sea, you know that it is "upcasting" for snow. It is a grand but a sinister sight, this army of giant clouds, crowding upon one another, lifting their rounded edges to be lighted up, for a short time, by the the setting sun, and then, when the western gleam has gone, becoming cold and grey, but not less threatening of approaching storm.

Although living many years in this far north corner of England, I have never heard my parishioners speak of lightning. Lightning with them is "fire." Thunder is regarded with much more awe than it is in the south; indeed, by many it is counted as the voice of God. And however bad the storm, it is the thunder that is spoken of. "Did you hear the 'thunner'?" the "fire" is not alluded to unless it is very vivid. A peal or clap of thunder is a "brattle" of "thunner." When our weather is doubtful and threatening at any season of the year, it is said to be "working for a change"; and when snow or rain is imminent, they say there is going to be "oncome." When the weather is dry with a wind which takes the moisture from the ground, it is "spiry."

The expression "mothy" weather applies to close, foggy and damp weather, the worst for harvest, spoiling the colour of the barley more than heavy rain, which runs off.

The use of "fore end" and "back end" for the beginning and close of the year is general here, also the "fall of the leaf" for autumn, and the "rise of the leaf" for spring. I was struck with the latter expression when a woman, whose son was delicate, told me he was always worse at the "rise of the leaf."

The curious old saw about the first three days of April being borrowed from April by March, is still on the lips of our old folks, and, by the way, April is always pronounced Apri-ill.

"Mairch borrow' it fra Apri-ill
Three days and they were ill."

March is personified as desiring to extend its wintry power for days, and for this purpose borrows them from April. According to an old Scottish rhyme, which I quote from Mr R Oliver Heslop's *Northumberland Words*, this borrowing by March is for a malicious and destructive purpose :---

"March said to Apriil,
I see three hoggs upon a hill,
And if you'll lend me dayes three,
I'll find a way to make them dee.
The first o' them was wind and weet,
The second o' them was snaw and sleet,
The third o' them was sic a freeze,
It froze the birds' nebs to the trees;
When the three days were past and gone
These three silly hoggs came hirpling hame."

(note, a hog is a one-year old sheep,
 neb means beak, or nose,
 hirpling, walking lame, limping)

The following extracts from *Wanderings in Spain*, by Augustus Hare, shows that this curious bit of weather lore exists, but in a somewhat different form, in Spain. The Spanish version represents March with the same malicious character, but it helps to clear up the difficulty of our version, by showing that six days were involved, the three last of March, and also the three first of April:---

"For the last few days of March it was very wet and stormy. They say it is always so in Spain, and concerning this there is an old Spanish story. A shepherd once said to March that if he would behave well he would make him a present of a lamb. March promised to deserve it, and conducted himself admirably. When he was going out, he asked the shepherd for the promised lamb, but the sheep and the lambs were so very beautiful, that the shepherd, considering that only three days of restraint remained to March, answered that he would not give it to him. 'You will not give it me,' said March, 'then you do not recollect that in the three days which remain to me and three days which my comrade, April, will lend me, your sheep will have to bring forth their young'; and for six days the rain and cold were so terrible that all the sheep and all the lambs died."

A storm of snow or sleet at the beginning of April is with us called a "Peez-weep storm," as it comes about the time when the "Peez-weeps" or lapwings lay their eggs in the fields. This local name better represents their peculiar cry as they circle over the land, than the name of Pee-wit. What infinite pains they take to deceive the passer-by, alighting anywhere but on the place where they have laid their eggs; and how hard it is for any but an experienced hand to find the eggs.

There are two or three home trades still existing in our village. Handsome and substantial willow baskets are made by the castle gardeners for use in their work, and the men who sweep the drives and walks in the grounds make their own brooms or "buzzoms" as they call them. These are of two kinds, the ordinary round broom like a bundle of sticks, formerly made of heather but now of birch, and the flat fan-shaped broom for sweeping up dried leaves. The latter are kept in their flat spreading shape by a band of iron not far below the handle. (Note, there is a public house at Coldstream called the "Besom" Hotel).

Until the other day I never beard of a scythe "strake." It appears that before the use of the whetstone, which makes so pleasant a sound in summer against the scythe where that time-honoured implement is not quite supplanted by the lawnmower, a sort of wooden strop called a "strake" was used for sharpening. This wooden sharpener had to he smeared over with fine sand to make it effective. The sand our villagers used for this purpose was fetched in carts from Cuddy's Cove, in the Kyloe Hills. This is a hollow or cave on the west side of a range of heather-covered hills, between Wooler and the coast. For some reason it is associated with St. Cuthbert. He may, in his preaching tours, have made it a temporary hermitage, for it is within a few miles of his monastery on Lindisfarne, which, with the Farne Island where he died, are clearly seen from the higher ground. (Note that a donkey is on the Border called a cuddy, and I believe in the North only, and is so-called because St. Cuthbert is supposed to have ridden one on his journeys).

The sitting hen is the "clocker"; a four pronged fork is a "grape"; to dig is to "howk"; a cow house is a "byre" a mole is a "moudiwarp"; a kitten is a "kitling." To select or choose, say, the large potato for sale or household use, and the small for the pig, is to "wale" them. Refuse, when used as a noun for useless material, is pronounced like the verb to refuse. Rushes used for thatching your hay, when straw is scarce, are always "rashers"; the shafts of a cart are "limmers"; and the horse that jibs is "reested." A lane or by-road is always a "lonnin" or "loanin." This word is also applied to the place near a village where the cows are got together at milking time. The word appears in Jean Elliot's beautiful version of the "Flowers of the Forest," which she composed with reference to the sad result of the Battle of Flodden and which may well be quoted here as this is within sight of Flodden Field.

"I've heard them liltin', at the ewe milkin',
Lasses a-liltin' before the dawn of day;
But now they are moanin' on ilka green loanin';
The Flowers of the Forest are a' wede away.

"We'll hear nae mair liltin' at the ewe milkin',
Women and bairns are heartless and wae;
Sighin' and moanin' on ilka green loanin'
The Flowers of the Forest are a' wede away."

A curious word is still in use implying secrecy. It is "under-hidlings." The people here define it as doing a thing known only to yourself. "Clashing" is gossiping. "Clishmaclash" means gossip or idle talk bandied about. "Castin' up" is reproaching. "Cruse" is lively, talking big, full of fun. "Glaikit" is, as we say, "not all there." "Kenspeckle" means well known. "Sweer" means averse to do a thing. "Bid" is always used for invite. After a death some person in each village is appointed to "bid" the people to the funeral. It is a rigid matter of etiquette never to attend a funeral, even of one you have known for years, unless you are bidden; and unless it is understood that the funeral is to he quite private it is considered a slight to omit anyone at all known to the deceased.

A very general form of greeting is "What fettle ?" meaning how are you? Do not trouble yourself or be anxious, is "Dinna' fash yersell"; "wyse a quit" is for leave go. "Bide a wee" for wait a little; while "Tak yer hook" is a way of saying take yourself off.

The word "friend" with us always means a relative. It is never used as in the south of a person with whom we are only in friendship. He is a "friend " of mine needs always the question, "Is he your uncle? Is he your cousin? What relation is he to you?"

To find fault with a person is to "quarrel" that person, the original meaning being to shoot an arrow at an enemy. You are not speaking the language of the countryside if you say of anything, I could not do without it. You must say, if you want to be understood, "I couldna' do wantin' it." I think it will rain must be "I doubt it will rain."

From the way in which our villagers and hinds speak of one another it is quite easy to realize how surnames originated. Their universal practice of calling their neighbours by their Christian names is very marked. To a stranger to the district this custom leads to the impression that there exists an unusual degree of brotherly and kindly feeling amongst them. Whether this be so or not, the habit is a clear indication of the predominance of the Christian name over the surname, and shows, to this day, that the latter was an adjunct of the former, given over and above. To this day the habit of past ages still exists with us of calling men by their trades, and dropping the family name altogether. There is still John the Smith, Billoby (William George) the Tailor, as there was seventy years ago Bell the Hind, Peter the Brewer, and Jack the Weaver. The last, however, had also another very significant surname. He was known to all the village lads as Jack the Leash, because he was much beset by them, and used often to run out and lay about him with a whip that had a long and stinging lash. His thatched cottage still exists opposite the school. Jack the Leash used not only to weave woollens and lint, but long poems on local events, bringing in in a galloping rhyme, descriptions of all his neighbours in connection with the sports of the district. It was rather curious also that the wife always shared the trade name with her husband. Thus, the weaver's wife was "Peg the Leash"; and "Ruth the Brewer" was the wife of "Peter the Brewer"; and "Nan the Tailor" was the wife of "Sam the Tailor, and so on. Such a name as Jock o' Yeavering shows how easily place names may even in our day become surnames. The very old custom of naming men according to their personal and physical peculiarities in the case of the same Christian and surname in different families was, until very lately, still in use. There were Black Matt, Red Matt, Fair Matt, all members of the same tribe in different generations. It is strange that

131

while the name Alexander as a Christian name is either pronounced as it is written or contracted into Alick when it is a surname it is always pronounced Elshner, but spelt Elshander, Alexander is too difficult to say.

Chapter XVII

Tales of the Countryside

In one outlying hamlet of the parish is a tumble-down row of red-tiled cottages, not considered worth repairing. One cottage was used as a chapel for Wesleyan local preachers, and others who felt moved to hold forth to their neighbours. An old collier, I well remember, frequently preached. On one occasion his subject was "Conscience," and he was illustrating it from his own experience. "Once, " said he, "I was in want of some nails, and considering how I should get them, I remembered I had seen a bag of nails in the weed shed of H----- Farm. Well, I went along to the farm, and sure enough, there was the bag of nails. There was nobody by, so I laid hands on the bag, and thinks I, 'six won't be no harm to take, and won't be missed. It won't be no loss,' for the bag was pretty full. It cannot he stealing to 'lift' six. So I took them out and into my pocket, looking round to see that the farmer was'na by, nor none of the hands. Back off I goes up the fields, and freends, you ken the twa stiles. When I gets to the first, I hopped over, feared like, for I thought of them words I heard in the Church Sunday School from the ould vicar, about picking and stealing. Now them words kept working in my inside till I come to the top stile, but I couldna' gan over ; them nails, though they was only six, drawed me backwards like a magnet, and away I go back. . . . to put----"

Here a young lad cried out, "Aye, so ye're ga'n back to lift the whole lot."

A curate of my parish used to preach occasionally in another cottage fitted up for mission services, and the same old man attended. The clergyman happened to refer to the devil, and said something about going about seeking whom he might devour, when old John cried out "Bind him, Lord, bind him." I fully believe the old man was a good Christian in his way, but he was so much in the habit of talking in theological language, and seemed so familiar with the Deity, that his conversation and frequent ejaculations had very much the effect of profanity.

Another old man in the same village, also a collier, was rather a remarkable character. When past work, he absolutely declined to leave the cottage he and his family had lived in for many years. His

133

wife and daughters were obliged to get their own living, and were employed on a neighbouring farm, where it was necessary for them to live. Nothing could induce old Willy to leave the cottage, which he had rent free from the proprietor. There he stayed alone for years nursing his rheumatism, sitting on a high-backed chair by a fire, which he supplied by gathering small bits of coal from heaps of refuse near disused coal shafts. When asked why he did not go to live with his family he said, "I canna be fashed with the wimmen folk."

I once remarked that it must be very lonely for him in his cottage, especially as he often sat up all night in pain, but his answer, which I am sure was given in no canting or irreverent spirit, was this---- "No, sir, I never feel dull. I'm aye divartin' mysel' convarsing with th' Almighty."

The King of the Gipsies used to come to our colliery, and always thought he had a royal right to have his cart at the head of the rank, but a giant at the pit village determined to cure the King of this. So one day he seized him, took him to the mouth of the shaft, and held him over the pit and kept him in this position until he promised that in future he would take his turn with others. Sometimes more than fifty carts would be waiting their turn.

The said giant once at Sunderland was known to lift an anchor that usually required six men to lift. When seized by a press gang, and taken on board a boat, he placed his back against one side and his feet against the other and split the boat in two.

Traditions of the press gang here are naturally few, and indistinct. It is evident, however, that tho village was sometimes times visited by man-of-war's men to effect their purpose. For I am told that Ford men used to lay themselves down on the roof of the public house to conceal themselves. There is an old rhyme in the minds of the people which runs:---

> Dance the tittery-tan, Marjorie,
> Dance the tittery-tan,
>   Yonder is the tender,
>   Coming to take our men.

This song was the accompaniment to a dance, in which the girls of the village went from house to house, as a signal to let the men know of the approach of the press gang. I had this from a very old man who died some years ago in Australia, but who was a native of our village.

Two women had neighbouring rigs in the village allotment ground. They had grown wheat upon them, and it was ripe for the harvest. People were "hard wrought" in those days, and time was precious; so one of these women went out on a bright moonlight night to shear her corn. As she worked, she now and then encroached a little on her neighbour's rig, for as much as would make a band to tie her sheaves. She went home, glad that the work was done. But on the next day, returning to the field, she found, to her chagrin, that she had mistaken her strip, and had reaped her neighbour's corn. The corn she had stolen to bind her sheaves was from her own rig, which it still remained for her to shear.

Sometimes banns of marriage are withdrawn before the last time of asking. I was once walking down a hill near my church when I met a woman bustling up in a great hurry. She said she wanted to see me. I said "About what?" She said, "About them banns; you're not to read them no more." Not knowing the woman, I said "What authority have you for taking the name off? " She answered, "I'm the woman herself." This, of course, was conclusive, and the banns were withdrawn.

A neighbouring clergyman relates, that after a funeral he had just taken, the person whose relative had been buried, formally proposed to the company of mourners that, before they dispersed, "a hearty vote of thanks" should be given to the vicar "for so kindly laying away his wife's mother."

One of the members of our St. Cuthbert's Clerical Society, who lived twelve miles from the place of meeting, was driving home in his little pony carriage, when he was accosted by a farmer who asked him for a lift. On reaching the farmer's house the farmer was full of gratitude for the kindness shown him, and begged that the clergyman would come in and partake of his hospitality. As it was rather late, my friend declined. The farmer expressed himself very puzzled how to make a return for the kindness of the clergyman, saying, "Well sir, all I can say is, there's a text which says, 'Vengeance is mine, I will repay saith the Lord.' " Our Border people have a very strong idea that for a favour given or received there should invariably be some return.

A man was arrested at Kelso for stealing a quantity of linen.

Before the trial came on he saw the lawyer whom he had engaged to defend him, and freely owned his guilt, and stated that he had the linen in his possession. "Go," said the lawyer, "and bring me a few yards of the linen." The trial came on, and it might have been observed that the lawyer for the defence made a rather fine display of shirt front, of which he seemed complacently proud.

The case for the prosecution was duly stated, and there seemed ample evidence of the man's guilt, but the defence, which proved to be very brief, was yet to come. It consisted of but one question addressed to the plaintiff by the defendant's counsel. Begging him to examine the texture of his shirt front, the Advocate asked if the stolen linen was of the same kind and quality? "No," said the man, "it was entirely different." The lawyer then explained to the court that the shirt was made out of a piece of linen that was found in the accused man's possession, but the plaintiff had proved that it was not the linen which had been stolen from him. He thus gained his case and his client was acquitted.

James Nevins, who is a hedger by trade, tells me that he was one evening at dusk working near a newly laid hedge that had a sheep-net in front, to protect it, when, all at once, he saw some object move to and fro before the hedge with amazing rapidity. He wondered much what it might be, and, on going towards the hedge, saw that it was a fox, which had already bitten through all the entanglement of the net, but the cord which still held one hind leg. When he got near it, the fox lay down as if dead. Nevins said, "Well, I shall have to let you away, but I'll go to the house and fetch something." He went and asked a neighbour for a wide-pronged hay fork. With this he pinned the head of the fox gently but firmly to the ground, without injuring him, and then took a knife, lifted up his leg, and cut away the cord. On releasing him, the fox although somewhat lamed ran off for a few yards, then turned round, sat on its hind-legs, looked in his face for a few moments, and then went off.

A very sad suicide had occurred in a neighbouring parish, and I had been visiting the house. The poor man took his life when in a state of depression, owing to the death of his wife, for whom he had a great affection, such as is not usual to show outwardly among our Border people, who are of such a very reserved nature. Indeed, any show of great affection between man and wife is often regarded by

136

them as a subject of jocose criticism. On my way home in calling at another cottage I was speaking of the incident, and expected my hearer to be sympathetic, but he only remarked, "Yes, sir, some carries it that far."

I was once going to a Visitation at Berwick. It was not intended for the clergy ; the Archdeacon was not there, but the Chancellor of the Diocese took his place. His duty was to meet the churchwardens and to swear them in, and receive the fees paid by them for the several parishes which they represented. I travelled in the train with one churchwarden of a neighbouring parish, who had held his office for a great number of years, and took a great pride in it. When we arrived at the vestry of Berwick Church, and the old gentleman had paid his fees to the Chancellor, who looked very formidable in his wig and gown, the Chancellor remarked to the assembled church wardens, "Gentlemen, I shall not deliver my charge to you to-day, but I will send it to you by post." "And when you do," said my aged friend, looking hard at the barrister, "tell us what you do with the money ?"

I once heard a story of churchwardens attending a Visitation at Belford. The clergy had been dining at the expense of the Archdeacon, but the churchwardens, as was then usual by way of encouraging the laity, were left out in the cold, and had to provide dinner for themselves. After they had dined one said to the other, "What did you think of the Archdeacon's charge?" The other thinking of the bill he had just paid, replied, "Exorbitant!"

A somewhat eccentric old lady thought she had been neglected by her doctor, whom she liked to see occasionally, whether she was ill or well. After brooding over this one day, she resolved to pay out the doctor for his neglect, by giving him what our people call "a gliff" (a fright). Having previously sent a peremptory message to the doctor to say that she was seriously ill, and begging him to come at once, she arranged the hall of her house as if for a funeral, hung the hall and furniture with white, placed a table in the centre, and laid herself out upon it, her servant covering her over with a white sheet. When the doctor arrived, and the servant with a sad countenance opened the door and admitted him, he exclaimed with awe-struck expression, "Is it come to this?" He then went up reverently to the table, lifted the corner of the sheet from the lady's face, when suddenly, to his great horror and amazement, she started

137

up, and reproached him for his neglect.

A vicar of Ellingham some years ago had the misfortune to fall over a sunk fence at the bottom of his garden, and to hurt himself very much. He called for help, and his gardener, who was not far off, heard him distinctly, but did not go to his assistance. When asked the reason of such strange conduct, he replied that "he didn't care to be mixed up with it."

It was at a time when many of the country clergy had to go to visitations, carrying their clerical vestments on their shoulders. Vicar Jenkinson, who was a well-known character, was once walking to Wooler with a brother priest. They got into a heated discussion, which culminated in a dispute as to which was the better man, and they agreed that at the next gate they would put it to the proof. When they came to the gate, they put down their belongings, took off their coats, and had a fierce pugilistic encounter, Parson Jenkinson overthrowing his enemy completely in the third round, and showing himself the better man. He was a man of some ability and culture. He was greatly interested in fossils, which at that time were found in the lime quarries near Lowick. Of these he made a large and valuable collection which afterwards, I believe, became the property of the University of Oxford.

A friend who was schoolmaster in Jenkinson's parish tells me Vicar Jenkinson was very fond of wrestling (short grips), and often he would ask a caller to try a throw with him, retiring behind the church to enjoy it. He was a formidable opponent, a St Bees' man, familiar with Border sports.

One day taking a walk he came upon a farmer and a horse-couper having a deal. He stopped, as he saw the farmer was about to buy, the couper assuring him that the horse was only about seven years old. "Let me look at his teeth," said the vicar. Having done so he exclaimed, "He was in the ark with Noah." The couper was very angry, but received the reply, "I am protecting one of my parishioners from imposition." "And I will pay you out for it," said the couper, beginning to put off his coat. In a second the vicar's coat was in the hands of the farmer, but the couper refused to close, knowing well the fame of his opponent as an athlete.

On coming one Sunday afternoon out of church after service in his surplice, there was a drunken disturbance among some Irish returning from harvesting. The vicar went amongst them to quiet

138

the disturbance. Grasping the ringleader by the nape of the neck he informed him that he would put him out of his parish. He pushed the man along a considerable distance, when the man gave in, and did not return.

So popular was Vicar Jenkinson with his parishioners, that on his return home, after two years' suspension from his benefice, he was met by a large crowd, who removed the horse and drew the carriage to his house.

Country post offices have undergone some improvement of late years, but they are even now far from what they should be. Owing to the extreme parsimony of the postal department, and the miserable way in which their servants are paid, our present advantages are not great, but they are a decided improvement on the past, as perhaps the following sketch will show.

Eliza had a supreme contempt for the public, and looked upon her postal duties as entirely subsidiary to her own affairs, especially the care of her cow. She was indeed a relic of old times, and was allowed to retain the office of post-mistress out of consideration for her feelings and circumstances. Haste is not a characteristic of our people, but nothing would induce Eliza to hurry; indeed, during the middle of the day, the post office was usually locked up, as then she was down at the byres fettling her cow.

An Inspector once arrived when she was thus engaged, and finding the door locked, went to seek her. He met her returning, and to his expostulation, she indignantly replied, "the cow must have her drap watter." Postal orders were a serious trial to her, as they required stamping as well as signing; but parcels were her special affliction, as they needed weighing. She had, however, a use of her own for the post office weights. Her grandfather clock it seems had none. Naturally, it annoyed her when people came with parcels. "Your clock is slow," someone innocently remarked " And well it might be," she replied ; "she's no chance with so many o' them parcels coming in."

YETHOLM GIPSIES

A former woodman on the Ford Estate was in his younger days a constable. Together with the Wooler constable, it was his duty to watch the gipsy poachers. On one occasion they had to go to

Yetholm, the gipsy village, to arrest one of the tribe. They thoroughly searched the man's house, which seemed quite empty, but before leaving, one of them felt under the bedclothes of the bed, and finding it warm, knew that his man could not be far off. Looking towards the chimney, they saw his feet hanging down. He had expended his strength in clinging to the chimney, and hastily descended and surrendered himself. He gave his word to the constables that he would not run away if they released their hold of him. This done, he said, "Run for your lives, for if I lift my hand all the others will be upon you." They discreetly took his advice, and left their errand unaccomplished. But the Yetholm gipsies at that time were a desperate lot, constables and game-keepers had dangerous work in dealing with them.

As an instance of the effect of a scientific lecture in the country, I may mention the following remark of a young man after attending one that was illustrated with experiments: "I dinna ken whether it was oxygen or nitrogen, but 'twas a kind o' yellowish colour, na reeck ye ken ; he jist poored it amang some other stufe, an' it a' went aff in a sort o' blue lour."

There was a curious custom in our Border villages of electing a man to be mayor of the village. This man was put into a cart and pulled about by his neighbours. It is true this custom was debased by a good deal of drinking and the mayor was, 1 believe, the greatest drunkard of all, and partly chosen on this account. Old men still talk of the Mayor of Ford, and we find in *Bishop Creighton's Life*, vol. i., that there was the same custom in Embleton, which is a far cry from Ford. Lowick also had its mayor. It would be interesting to know whether this election of mayors in villages had its origin in the days when there were village communities, with headmen to look after their interests.

A well-to-do farmer returning from market was drowned in fording the Tweed near Wark, and although every effort was made, his body was not found. Some months afterwards a man belonging to Norham, who was an elder of the church, saw the body of a dead man, partly covered with sand, at the side of the Tweed, evidently washed down by a flood. He took it out, robbed it of a large sum of money, and placed it again as he had found it. On looking up he saw that his evil deed had been observed, for there was a tramp on the bank watching him. Instantly filled with dread of discovery, and determined to keep his ill gotten gold, he sprang at the tramp, and with a savage blow on the head, with a heavy stick, brought him to the ground, and afterwards killed him, and threw him in the stream. His crime was never discovered. He lived to be an old man much respected by his neighbours. In his last illness, he was, as it were, dead several times, but always revived again. As the saying goes "he could not die." This gave much concern to his neighbours. One old body came in convinced that his lingering death showed that there was something on his mind that needed confessing, and said, "In the name of God, unburden your conscience." He then told her the story of his crime, and died soon after.

THE STORY OF PHILADELPHIA.

Every river valley in our land collects about itself a thousand traditions, but the greater number are carried away by time like the drift-wood gathered by the stream, and borne outward to the ocean. It need hardly be said that few river valleys are richer in tragic and romantic incident than the valley of the Tweed.

One glance at the splendid mass of Norham's ruined keep, standing out sentinel-like against the North, is enough to tell the tale.

The incidents of Border warfare have long since given place to those of a more homely character, but there is about them quite as much of human interest.

About a hundred and fifty years ago the vicar of the fine old church at Norham was a Mr. Robert Lambe. Of a scholarly disposition, and dwelling in the heart of a district full of historic associations, he took up the study of the Ballad poetry of the North, and edited the fine old poem of "Flodden Field," which at the time was little known. Engrossed in these and other studies, he remained a bachelor for many years, until his friends deemed it expedient that a wife should be found for him. He listened to their advice, and bethought him of an old acquaintance, a carrier in Durham: he knew that he had a daughter, but had not seen her since she was a small child. It would be a simple matter, he thought, for her to come in one of her father's wagons from Durham to Berwick, a journey that otherwise would be formidable.

141

This excellent plan was carried out. The proposal was sent to the young lady, who, it is said, was very charming, and rejoiced in the old-world name of Philadelphia, and was accepted, with the consent of her father, who was in no wise averse to so eligible a match for his daughter; for the vicarage of Norham was one of the choice benefices in the patronage of St. Cuthbert's Dean and Chapter.

As the two were unacquainted with one another, and Philadelphia was to arrive unaccompanied by any relative who knew Mr. Lambe, it was necessary that some preconcerted signal should be agreed upon which would enable her future husband to identify her. He was to meet her on an appointed day and hour on Berwick Pier, and she was to walk there carrying a tea-caddy under her arm. The wagon duly arrived, and the lady, but no clergyman came to welcome her and help her to alight. But the Pier was the appointed place of meeting, so to the Pier she found her way, and began to walk up and down, with a strange feeling of trepidation, expecting every moment to see her friend approaching.

Now there was an old gentleman whose custom it was to take a walk on the Pier three times daily. During one of his morning walks he took casual notice of a pretty girl walking along holding a tea-caddy, as if it were a thing of importance. After an early dinner he took his second walk, and was surprised to see the same girl looking fagged and disconsolate. He thought it very strange, but with North country reserve and reluctance to meddle with other people's business, he passed by. On going out for his third walk, however, his reserve was quite overcome. He again saw the girl, this time in tears, worn out with fatigue, and seated on one of the benches of the Pier, with the tea-caddy still in her hands. He ventured to ask what was the matter, and if he could be of any service. The answer came in tones of wounded pride, and petulance. "I came to be married to the Vicar of Norham - he promised to meet me here, but has never come."

"It will be all right," said the stranger, "the Vicar of Norham is a friend of mine. Come to my house until tomorrow and we will send to fetch him. He's an old bookworm, and has forgotten all about it." Such was the case.

Vicar Lambe, however, was soon on the spot, reconciliation was effected, and the marriage took place, the bridegroom's present to his wife being a silver teapot. Among the descendants of Mr.

Lambe "Philadelphia" is a favourite name, and a teapot is always presented to the one who bears it.

An inhabitant of Coldstream tells me that the Tweed is the boundary between England and Scotland from Carham, but is, nevertheless, a Scotch river from bank to bank. Indeed, there is still a field on the south side, not far from Cornhill in the flat land bordering the river, which is actually a part of Scotland. A man was once taken up and tried at Berwick for infringing the fishing laws at that spot. He pleaded in defence that he was on Scottish land when he committed the act, and claimed that he could not justly be tried in an English court, and so got off.

There seems to me strong ground for the belief that the Tweed in this part, at some very distant period, altered its course, coming south of Wark Castle, instead of north of it as before. At the foot of a hill bounding the flat land to the south of the river there is some land called Dry Tweed, which is crossed by the little stream called the Lear. There is a farm there called Learmouth; and it looks as if the mouth of the Lear was once at that point, some distance inland from the Tweed.

Calling at a cottage some years ago I remarked to the woman of the house on the pleasant sound of the striking of her eight-day clock-----she accounted for its musical tone by saying that she once lived near Dryburgh at a time when a portion of one of the ancient bells of the Abbey was dug up near the walls of that lovely ruin. Somehow a fragment of the metal came into possession of her husband. It was melted down and made into a bell for her clock, so that we may say that the silvery sound of Dryburgh's Abbey bells is heard on the Border to this day.